Beginner's Guide to
SILK
PAINTING

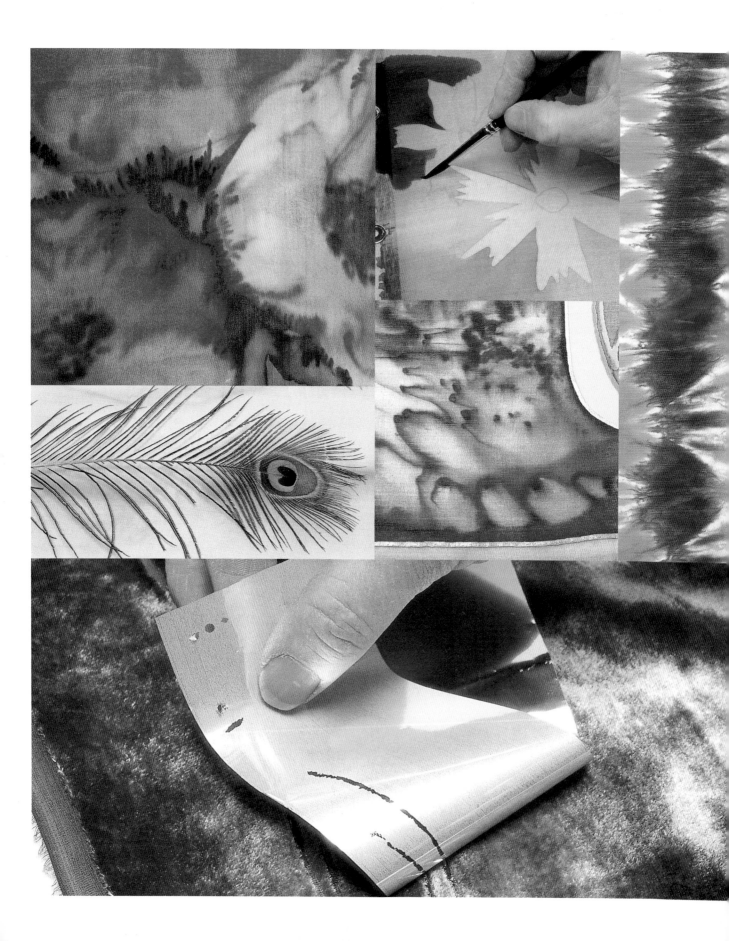

Beginner's Guide to
SILK
PAINTING

CAROLINE EARL

Sterling Publishing Co., Inc.
New York

Creative director: Sarah King
Editor: Judith Millidge
Project editor: Sally MacEachern
Designer: 2H Design

Library of Congress Cataloging-in-Publication Data Available

10   9   8   7   6   5   4   3   2   1

Published in 2003 by Sterling Publishing Co.,Inc.
387 Park Avenue South, New York, N.Y. 10016

This book was designed and produced by
D&S Books Ltd.
Kerswell, Parkham Ash,
Bideford, Devon, EX39 5PR, U.K.

Distributed in Canada by Sterling Publishing
C/o Canadian Manda Group,
One Atlantic Avenue, Suite 105
Toronto, Ontario, Canada M6K 3E7

Printed in Singapore

Sterling ISBN 1-4027-0879-3

Contents

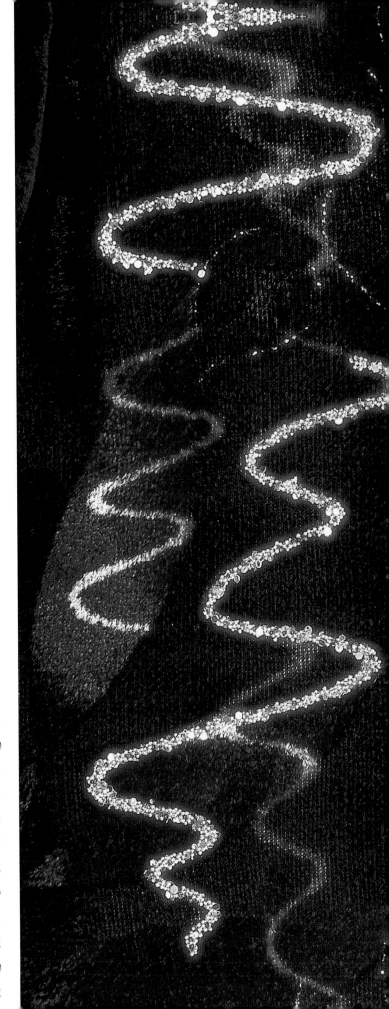

Introduction

Silk painting is a fascinating and beautiful medium. With the versatility of various silk dyes, paints, and other media that form the palette of the silk painter or textile artist, it is possible to create a wide range of effects and styles. The tactile qualities of textiles and the vibrant colors of this medium are absorbing and inspiring. Silk painting provides endless possibilities for creating unique pieces of decorated silk, which can be made up into many decorative and functional items. The personal satisfaction gained from an admired scarf, or a compliment from the recipient of a painting or card gives enormous pleasure to the artist and inspires one to do more.

his book introduces a range of techniques that are both fun and
sy. Many varied ways of applying the silk dyes, paints, and
ediums are clearly explained, with information on the
uipment and materials you will need to start. Suggestions and
formation on color, how to work up designs, and a selection of
tterns and projects are included to help get you started,
llowed by advice on how to advance and extend your silk-
inting skills.

hope you find pleasure in working through this book, whether
a beginner or as a keen silk painter looking for further
spiration. For the complete beginner, I add a few words of
ution—be warned, silk painting is very addictive!

The Historical Production of Silk

Sericulture, or the production of silk, has been practiced for thousands of years. China, India, and other Far
Eastern countries produced and wove silk fabrics that were highly regarded and the prized possessions of
emperors, royalty, and the most wealthy members of society. Silk weaving in Britain did not become
particularly important until the 16th and 17th centuries, when weavers came across from the Low Countries
and France, where there was already an established silk-weaving industry. These immigrant silk weavers
initially settled in London, particularly around Spitalfields, and gradually spread across to other areas of
the country. Silk weaving quickly became an important and specialized trade, resulting in the
foundation of the Guild of Silkweavers in 1629.

Silk comes from the fine filaments or fibers that form the cocoon of the silk moth.
Wild silk moths are found in many different countries, but many hundreds of years
ago the Chinese recognized the special qualities of the fine silk filament
produced from the *Bombyx mori* silkworm. The cultivated silkworm of
the *Bombyx mori* silk moth produces a filament that is more round in
shape and smoother and finer than other silk moths', which
makes it easier to unwind and work into a stronger thread
and fabric.

The female silk moth lays 400–500 tiny eggs. In the
late spring, the eggs start to hatch, and a new
generation of silk producers emerge. These tiny
silkworms feed entirely on mulberry leaves, and
rapidly mature over the next four to five
weeks, outgrowing and shedding their skin
around four times. When the adult silkworm reaches
3–4 in. (7.5–10 cm) long , it stops feeding and begins to spin its
cocoon. It can use over a mile (up to 2 kilometers) of silk filament to produce the

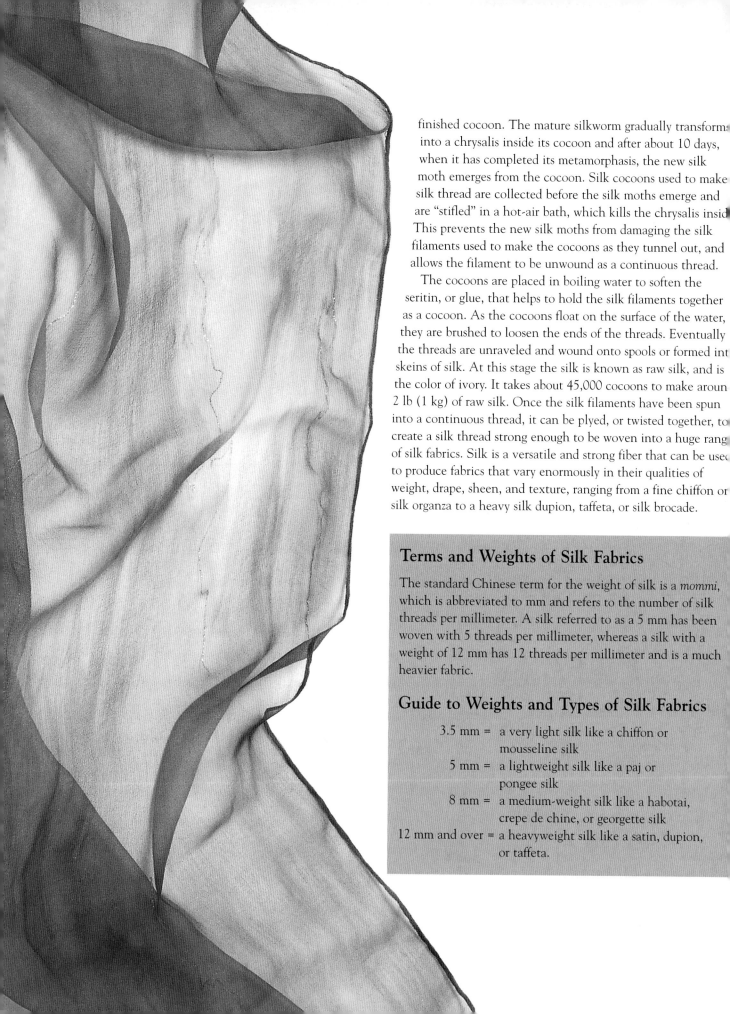

finished cocoon. The mature silkworm gradually transforms into a chrysalis inside its cocoon and after about 10 days, when it has completed its metamorphasis, the new silk moth emerges from the cocoon. Silk cocoons used to make silk thread are collected before the silk moths emerge and are "stifled" in a hot-air bath, which kills the chrysalis inside. This prevents the new silk moths from damaging the silk filaments used to make the cocoons as they tunnel out, and allows the filament to be unwound as a continuous thread.

The cocoons are placed in boiling water to soften the seritin, or glue, that helps to hold the silk filaments together as a cocoon. As the cocoons float on the surface of the water, they are brushed to loosen the ends of the threads. Eventually the threads are unraveled and wound onto spools or formed into skeins of silk. At this stage the silk is known as raw silk, and is the color of ivory. It takes about 45,000 cocoons to make around 2 lb (1 kg) of raw silk. Once the silk filaments have been spun into a continuous thread, it can be plyed, or twisted together, to create a silk thread strong enough to be woven into a huge range of silk fabrics. Silk is a versatile and strong fiber that can be used to produce fabrics that vary enormously in their qualities of weight, drape, sheen, and texture, ranging from a fine chiffon or silk organza to a heavy silk dupion, taffeta, or silk brocade.

Terms and Weights of Silk Fabrics

The standard Chinese term for the weight of silk is a *mommi*, which is abbreviated to mm and refers to the number of silk threads per millimeter. A silk referred to as a 5 mm has been woven with 5 threads per millimeter, whereas a silk with a weight of 12 mm has 12 threads per millimeter and is a much heavier fabric.

Guide to Weights and Types of Silk Fabrics

3.5 mm =	a very light silk like a chiffon or mousseline silk
5 mm =	a lightweight silk like a paj or pongee silk
8 mm =	a medium-weight silk like a habotai, crepe de chine, or georgette silk
12 mm and over =	a heavyweight silk like a satin, dupion, or taffeta.

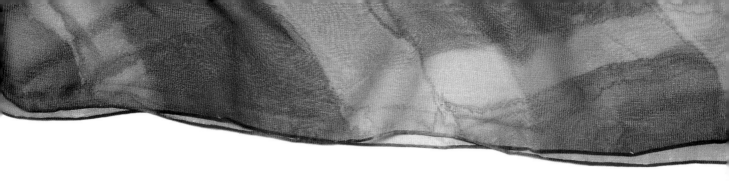

Materials and Equipment

You can start silk painting with basic equipment, although there are many items that can be gradually added to allow a more in-depth working of this versatile medium.

Safety

Even with something as seemingly harmless as painting, there are safety implications that should be noted. Most liquid silk dyes and paints are water-based and harmless, but procion powder dyes must be handled sensibly while they are in their powder form, so wear a mask when measuring out and mixing to avoid inhaling them. When handling any chemical, wear protective rubber gloves to avoid contact with the skin. This applies to soda ash, which is a strong alkaline solution, and fiber-etch solution, which could be irritating to the skin. Keep measuring spoons, utensils, bowls, jugs, and any other equipment needed for silk painting and dyeing separate from the items you use in the kitchen.

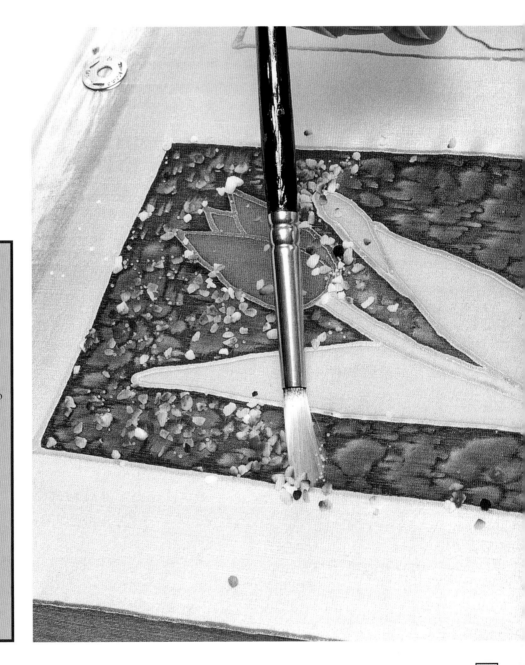

SILK

Lightweight pongee silk is an excellent weight for the beginner to work on. It is suitable for samplers and practice pieces, as well as cards, pictures, and scarves. As you become more skilled, try some of the other types and weights of silks.

Start with small frames and adjustable notched frames.

SILK PAINTS AND DYES

Buy a basic selection of silk paints and dyes. Further information on silk paints and dyes is given on page 14.

GUTTA AND OUTLINERS

Forming barrier lines to control the flow of the silk colors is a fundamental part of silk painting. Barrier lines are formed with gutta or silk-paint outliners, which come in tubes or plastic pipette bottles, and are available in a selection of colors.

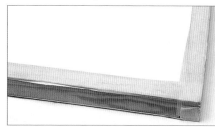

A fixed frame is easy to make yourself.

FINE METAL TIPS

Metal tips can be fitted onto the nozzle of the plastic applicator bottles to help control the resist line. Available in a selection of nib sizes from 0.3 mm to 1.00 mm, they come with a fine cleaning wire that helps stop the hole becoming blocked when it is not being used. Stick a small piece of masking tape to the end of the cleaning wire to mark the size of the tip and help prevent the loss of the fine wire if it is accidentally dropped onto the floor.

Sliding frames give good adjustability.

SILK-PAINT THICKENER

This is added to the silk paint or dye to change the way the color flows.

ANTISPREAD SOLUTION

This is applied to the silk to change the color-spreading qualities of the silk.

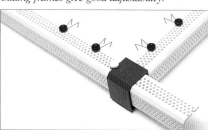

Holed frames give fine adjustability and have the

EFFECT SALTS

These are sprinkled onto the wet, colored silk to create texture patterns.

FRAMES

Most silk painting is done with the fabric supported on a frame, which stretches the silk and helps the dye to flow evenly. Frames can be as simple as an old wooden picture frame or four pieces of wood fastened together to make up a rigid square or rectangle. If you make your own frame, choose wood that is not too hard, so that the silk pins will easily push into it. A frame that allows some sort of adjustment is more efficient, both for stretching the silk and to accommodate different sizes of material. Frames can be made of wood, plastic, or metal. Investigate a selection of frames and see which type seems best.

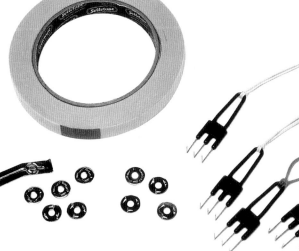

Silk pins, stenter pins, and double-sided tape.

[SI]LK PINS, STENTER PINS, AND DOUBLE-[SI]DED TAPE

[Si]lk pins are usually employed to fasten silk to a frame. The [sim]plest are three-pointed silk pins, which divide the fibers of [th]e material rather than making holes as the silk is tensioned. [Th]ese pins are made of steel and can rust if the salt-effect [cr]ystal deposits employed in some projects are not washed [of]f occasionally.

[St]enter, or claw, pins are an alternative to three-pointed pins. [St]enter pins are particularly useful for awkward-sized pieces or [wh]en if you want to paint right up to rolled edges on the silk. It [is] possible to create your own stenter pins (see page 23 for [in]structions). Some frames come with their own pins.

[D]ouble-sided tape is another alternative, and is good for [lar]ge areas of silk that do not have a ready rolled edge. See [pa]ge 22 for instructions on how to use this method of [ten]sioning the silk.

[P]AINTBRUSHES

[A] good selection of paintbrushes is essential, as they are the [m]ain tool for applying and moving the silk paints and dyes. [So]ft, round, watercolor brushes that form a good point, or [C]hinese brushes, are suitable.

[B]rush quality varies enormously, but spend as much as you [ca]n afford, and then make sure that you look after your brushes [pr]operly. Brush sizes between 2 and 12 are probably most useful [to] start with, plus a larger Chinese or foam brush for [ba]ckgrounds and large areas. Use old brushes, decorating [br]ushes, or hog brushes when working with wax.

[S]ilk dyes should not damage or stiffen brushes, but heat-fix [pa]ints can slightly stiffen brushes after a period of time. Use [yo]ur best brushes with steam-fix dyes, and save the second-best [fo]r heat-fix paints.

[M]IXING PALETTES, CUPS, SPRAY [B]OTTLES

[A] small, multiwelled mixing palette is essential for [si]lk painting. A good selection of wells will [en]courage color mixing, which adds far [m]ore variation and depth to your work. [F]or larger pieces of work or [ba]ckgrounds, plastic cups, jam jars, or [a] larger palette well are necessary to avoid [ru]nning out of color before the area is fully [co]lored. Palettes can be made of china or [pl]astic. Some paints and dyes can stain plastic palettes, although china palettes should not be affected. Pump-action spray bottles are very useful for spraying color or water. A large water pot is also essential. Change the water frequently as dirt on the brush will spoil the clarity of the colors.

PIPETTE DROPPERS

Plastic pipette droppers are useful for carefully lifting up color or water with the minimum of spillage. Most pipette droppers have marked graduations on the side, which allow accurate recording and remixing of colors.

PAPER TOWELING AND COTTON BUDS

Paper toweling or kitchen roll is essential for wiping the inevitable blob that forms at the beginning of the outliner tube when you first start silk painting, and for drying off the brush between rinses to keep the colors at the correct depth. Paper toweling can quickly absorb excess quantities of dye or water on the silk, and cotton buds are useful for small spaces.

SOFT PENCILS AND DISAPPEARING PENS

If you are not tracing from a pattern placed under the silk, use either a very soft 4B pencil or a disappearing pen to draw directly onto the silk. Disappearing pens are available as auto-fade pens whose ink vanishes after a period of time, or as water-soluble pens, where the ink disappears after contact with water.

Fixing equipment.

FIXING EQUIPMENT

Heat-fix silk paints are normally fixed by ironing. Use a flat iron in preference to a steam iron when heat-fixing. An iron is also used to remove any wax used as a resist on the silk. It is also possible to oven-cure heat-fix paints. Please refer to page 40 for further information on this process.

Other silk dyes are set by steam-fixing. The work is rolled up with wallpaper lining or cotton, which absorbs any excess dyes during the steaming process, and is then steamed in a saucepan or pressure cooker. See the section on steam-fix dyes on page 16 for further information.

HAIRDRYER

A hairdryer can speed up the process of drying outliners, water and color washes. It can also be used selectively to dry particular parts of a design or to help create watermarks.

SCISSORS

Use sharp scissors for cutting the silk and for careful trimming and finishing techniques.

METER RULE OR YARD STICK

This can be used to draw neat, straight gutta lines in a geometric design or to create a border. The ruler can also be used to help measure and calculate quantities required for a particular design or project.

PLASTIC CANVAS SQUARE

A 4 in. (10 cm) square of plastic canvas makes a simple measuring grid for quickly marking out even corner-point marks when creating a border design and is available from sewing or craft stores. Make a series of larger holes, at intervals of your choosing, on the diagonal line of the square. It can then be placed into each corner of your silk while it is stretched out on the frame and the corner points marked with a water-soluble pen or soft pencil in the appropriate hole to create a border of the required depth. The edges can also be used to mark out border widths. See page 46.

SYNTHRAPOL

This is a concentrated liquid detergent that can be added to the rinse water to help wash out loose dye particles from the silk. Please refer to the manufacturer's instructions for a guide on dilution rates.

PROTECTIVE CLOTHING

Wear rubber gloves to protect your skin, especially when using chemical-based mediums. It is also sensible to wear an apron because most paints and dyes have the capacity to stain clothing even before they are properly fixed.

BOWLS, SPOONS, JUGS, AND JAM JARS

Have a bowl, measuring jug, teaspoon, tablespoon, and a good collection of jam jars, preferably with screw-top lids, ready to use when measuring out, mixing up, and storing dyes. These should labeled and kept purely for craft purposes, not used in the preparation of food.

WAX

Wax is used as a resist or barrier and requires a few specialist pieces of equipment. Paraffin-wax granules are easier to use than blocks of wax as they can be topped up with additional granules more easily than breaking off a chunk of wax. Beeswax can also be added, which makes the wax more pliable and less likely to crackle. Wax should be melted in a thermostatically controlled wax pot. If this is not possible, use a double saucepan to melt the wax, checking that the water in the base does not dry out. Wax should never be left unattended while it is being heated, and should be placed in a safe place even while it is cooling down.

Wax is applied to the fabric with a tjanting, or canting, a traditional Javanese penlike tool. Available in a selection of styles and sizes, the bowl that holds the wax can be round or pointed. It is normally made from brass or copper, which retains the heat and helps to keep the wax molten. The fine spouts vary in size to produce lines of various widths, and there are double and triple cantings that produce several lines at once.

Wax pot, cantings, and wax.

...ongee white silk. ✗✗

...edevorée white silk satin.

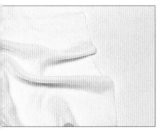

...hite velvet.

...k satin stripe, white.

...ack silk.

...repe de chine.

Predevorée white silk velvet.

Black velvet.

White jacquard pattern.

Chiffon.

Dupion silk. have this kind

SILK FABRICS SUITABLE FOR PAINTING

Despite the huge range of silk fabrics available, not all are suitable for painting by the inexperienced painter. As a general rule, you should initially avoid fabrics with an uneven surface, or slub in their weave, as it can be difficult to ensure that both the resist and dye have sufficiently penetrated the whole of the silk fabric. It is best to start working on smooth, evenly surfaced silks, like the pongee, paj, and habotai silks, which all enable the resist to seal the silk easily, and the silk dyes to move effectively across the surface.

✗✗ Pongee or habotai silk comes from China and is particularly good for the inexperienced silk painter. Available in a range of weights, it has a white, smooth, even surface, with a good sheen that helps to enhance the finished painting. Lightweight and inexpensive, it has a less tightly packed weave, so silk dyes spread very easily across the surface. A lightweight silk can be used for many projects: floaty scarves, hair ties, cards, pictures, and test pieces.

Medium-weight habotai silk has the same smooth surface, but is more dense in weave and has a slightly thicker thread, giving a stronger and heavier fabric. This weight is suitable for such projects as pillow covers, scarves, pieces where creative embroidery or quilting is to be added, or clothing where a less translucent appearance of the silk is required.

The heavyweight habotai silk provides a substantial fabric for use in upholstery projects, clothing, kimonos, and for screen panels, banners, and wallhangings. Any silk can be backed with another fabric or interfacing to add further strength, although bear in mind that the drape of the fabric will be affected.

✗✗ The heavier the weight of silk, the slower the dye will spread across its surface. This makes some silks, such as crepe de chine, more suitable for working designs without the use of a linear resist (a barrier to limit the spread of the dye). You may need to use more of a brushing action to distribute the color evenly, rather than relying on the silk's natural capillary action to spread the color across the surface of the stretched silk. Greater quantities of dye will be needed to penetrate and color all the fibers of the silk. However, once distributed, the color will appear slightly more intense on a heavier silk than on a lighter weight because the fabric is more dense in construction. ✗✗

Once you have done a few samplers and practice pieces on various weights of smooth-surfaced silks, you may like to try working on other types of silk. Silk velvet, silk satin, crepe de chine, jacquard, georgette, and chiffon silks are all suitable for painting, each offering different qualities to the finished piece of work.

Dab a spot of water onto the silk to test its flow qualities.

TESTING A PIECE OF SILK FOR PAINTING

Before starting work on a piece of silk, check whether it has an "dressing" in the surface that will impair the flow of the silk paint or dye. To test whether the silk is ready for painting, just dab a small spot of water on one corner and watch to see whether the water spreads out easily. If the spot of water sits on the surface like a small bead and does not sink into the silk or spread across the surface, the material contains some dressing that is preventing the absorption of the water. The silk must therefore be washed in hot, soapy water before being used for painting. However, if the spot of water sinks into the silk and spreads out freely and evenly, it is ready for working, as water reacts in the same way that the paints and dyes will spread.

Silk Paints and Dyes

A wide range of paints and dyes is available, although for the best results it is preferable to use ones that have been specifically formulated for use on silk fabrics. These allow the colors to be fixed permanently into the fabric using a variety of different methods.

With a wide selection of paints and dyes to choose from, choosing the most suitable can be confusing . Most people start with a heat-fix silk paint because of the simplicity of the fixing process and then progress to try steam-fix dyes, or possibly acid dyes and procion dyes. All of these types of paints color silk effectively and

permanently. It is often possible to substitute one dye type for another, so if you prefer to work with heat-fix paints, just substitute your preferred paints, taking into consideration any changes necessary for their particular working and fixing requirements.

It is not simply a case that one paint or dye is better than another. Each type is different, offering various qualities that could be beneficial to a particular type of silk or to the project being worked, or that may suit one person more than another. A silk paint or dye should therefore be selected on its suitability for the project being worked and the preferences of the individual artist.

A selection of silk paints and dyes.

note ↓

HEAT-FIX SILK PAINTS

e most frequently used paints are heat-fix, water-based,
ylic silk paints that can be intermixed with one another for a *not use*
de range of colors and diluted with water for paler tints.
ese are popular because they are easy to use and can be
ply fixed with the heat from an iron. Heat-fix silk paints
rk by coating the silk fibers rather than penetrating them,
d you can normally feel the difference between a silk paint
d a silk dye. Another quality of heat-fix paints is that they
nnot be further worked or moved into new patterns on the
k once dry, although further layers of paint can be applied on
. This means that achieving a constant, even color across a
ge area, such as a background, can be quite difficult for the
vice silk painter. With a heat-fix paint, if any part of the
a being painted dries before being completely painted, a
n mark, or watermark, is almost inevitable where the wet
nt meets the dry silk paint. Once dry, these paints are simply
d quickly fixed by ironing, which makes this silk paint the
al choice for the beginner or for work in schools or
rkshops where the length of the working sessions can be
important consideration.

ETTING HEAT-FIX PAINTS

oning

ne ironing process allows the acrylic binder and pigments to
nd onto the fibers, giving a durable and washable finished
oric. Iron fixing can be applied directly to the reverse of the
oric, or through a piece of paper or fine cotton fabric. Ironing
o sets the heat-fix outliners, which are intended to remain in
e fabric and so give a slightly textured finish to the silk. The
ly exception to this is the clear outliner, which is removed on
e initial washing of the fixed piece.
The reverse side of the fabric should be ironed because the
tliners sit slightly proud of the surface on the right side, but
e quite flat on the reverse of the fabric. Use a hot or wool
tting and give the piece a thorough ironing for two minutes,
eping the iron moving the whole time to avoid scorching any
ea of silk. If you detect any bubbling in the outliner, the iron
too hot, or has remained in one position for too long, or
ssibly the outliners were not completely dry and the heat
m the iron has caused uneven drying. Heat-fix silk paints are
w much improved and only give a very slight stiffening to the
nished fabric, which may decrease after a series of washes. X X

ry-curing ✓ *need parchment paper, xx*

is also possible to set heat-fix paints by gently heating the silk
a domestic oven, which is especially useful for large or

awkward-shaped items. Loosely fold the silk and place it on a
clean baking sheet. Very light or delicate silk can be covered
with baking paper. The silk can then be gently fixed in an
oven, at 275°F/140°C for 10 minutes, or tumbled in a tumble-
dryer for about 15 minutes. ✓

STEAM-FIX DYES

Steam-fix silk colors are dyes that penetrate and bond with the
whole fiber of the fabric, giving color without affecting the
softness or drape of the silk. Another advantage is that the
intensity of color is increased by the steam-fixing process. It is
possible to intermix colors, and pale hues can be achieved by
diluting the dyes with water or other dilutants. Unlike heat-fix
acrylic silk paints, steam-fix dyes have the capacity to reform
into different patterns on subsequent applications of dye or
water until they are fixed. This gives tremendous scope for
added patterning when working a design in a series of layers,
even if previous layers of dye have completely dried. Once the
fixing process has been applied, these dyes are also washable
and many can also be dry cleaned (but check the manufacturer's
care instructions).

ACID DYES *any of mine ?*

Acid dyes are easy to use and give brilliant colors. They are
suitable for dyeing wool, silk, and other protein-based fibers.
They are called acid dyes because they need hot, acidic
conditions to drive the dye into the fibers, which is most easily
achieved by using acetic acid or vinegar in combination with a
steam setting process. Steam setting is achieved in exactly the
same way as for steam-fix dyes (see page 16), with the addition
of a couple of tablespoons of vinegar in the water reservoir in
the bottom of the pan. They also work well in the microwave
techniques described on page 40.

HOW TO MIX UP POWDERED ACID DYES

Wearing a protective mask, carefully measure out one teaspoon
of dye powder and place it in a clean measuring jug with a small
quantity of hot, but not boiling, water. To achieve stronger
colors, increase the quantity of dye powder. Stir to dissolve the
dye powder, then add a further quantity of cold water to bring
the quantity up to 7 fl. oz (220 ml). Pour this liquid dye into a
screw-top jam jar for immediate use and short-term storage. Try
not to make more dye than you need for a particular project.
The acetic acid or vinegar will be added at the working stage if
using the microwave technique, or at the steam-fixing stage for
conventional steaming.

read
latter

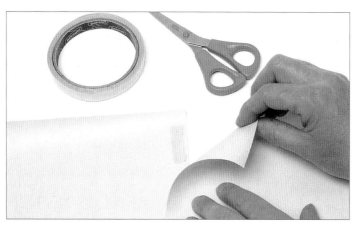

Joining and sticking fixing paper together with double-sided tape.

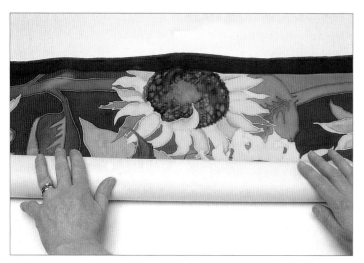

Rolling up the work in absorbent paper or cotton.

Coiling up the roll to fit into steaming pan.

Fixing Your Work

Once the dyes are dry and the design is complete, the silk must be steamed to make the colors fast and washable. There are various way of steaming the finished work that all follow the same procedure, but the container used and the time required to set the dyes may vary.

STEAM-FIXING USING A PRESSURE COOKER

Place the dried, unfixed, silk-painted pieces on some thin, cotton material or absorbent paper, such as wallpaper lining paper. Wallpaper lining may be too narrow for large pieces of silk, so simply join two strips together with a few short pieces of double-sided tape along the center overlap. As you lay out the finished work, make sure that there is a gap of about 2 in. (5 cm) between each piece, with a similar amount at the outer edges. This will prevent the pieces from touching each other as the work is rolled up.

Carefully roll up the unfixed pieces of silk, ensuring that the cotton fabric or absorbent paper is not creased. Try not to make the roll too tight; keep it loose and squashy so that it is easier to coil up and fit into a pressure-cooker pan. Seal up one end of the roll with tape and coil the roll, beginning with the sealed end. Secure, and seal up the other end of the completed coil with a few pieces of masking tape or sticky tape to prevent it from uncoiling. To ensure that the coil does not come undone during the fixing process, tie a piece of string around it, checking that there are no long ends of string that could trail into the water during the fixing. This coil shape is often referred to as a parcel.

Put ³/₄ in. (2 cm) of water in the base of the pressure-cooker pan and then place a trivet or stand in the base of the pan for the parcel to sit on. If you do not have a trivet, make one by folding a good length of aluminum foil into a stiff strip about 4 in. (10 cm) deep and coiling this up to form a stand. The parcel must not come into direct contact with the water.

Put the parcel on the trivet and place a domed hat, made of aluminum foil shaped over a pudding basin, on top of the parcel. This prevents any droplets of condensation from dropping from the lid of the pressure cooker onto the coil during steaming. It should be replaced as soon as small, pinprick holes appear in the foil after a couple of steamings. Using the complete pressure-cooker weights, place the lid of the pressure cooker on the base and close together.

Quickly bring the water to the boil to pressurize the pan, but ɔce the pan is pressurized (shown by the weight rattling or the ɯve coming up), reduce the heat right down to a simmer ɯting. This should be just sufficient to maintain the pressure, so ɔk for 20 minutes from this point. As a rough guide, 20 nutes is sufficient for up to an 8-foot running length of light-ɔ medium-weight silk or 2.5 meters of fabric. Should the ɔssure drop during this time, just increase the heat slightly and ɔ another few minutes.

After the correct cooking time, turn off the heat, or remove ɔ pressure cooker from the heat source, and allow the pressure ɔ drop. Once the pressure has dropped, you can safely open the ɔ of the pressure cooker and remove and unwrap the parcel ɔile it is still warm. If you have used water-based outliners, ɯays open the parcel while it is still warm as it is easier to ɔach any silk that has stuck to the paper during the fixing. If ɔ find that any pieces of silk are really stuck to the paper ɔough heavy usage of outliner, particularly on chiffon or ɔhtweight silk, do not try to force the silk away from the paper. ɔrefully tear the paper around the problem area, leaving the ɔer attached to the silk. Then place the silk, with the stuck ɔer still attached, into the rinsing water and gently agitate the ɔ. The water will quickly soften the water-soluble outliner and ɔs will allow the piece of paper to be removed without ɔnaging the silk.

Allow the fixed pieces to settle and cool down before washing ɔh piece of fixed silk in warm water with a little liquid ɔergent to remove any traces of water-soluble outliner, excess ɔor, or salt deposits. As the silk fabric can only absorb a given ɔntity of dye, any excess dye will sit on the surface of the ɔric and will be washed away at the rinsing stage, so do not be ɔrly concerned about a slight discoloration of the water. To ɔid staining the silk during the rinsing process, gently move it ɔund in the rinsing water rather than just leaving it to soak, so ɔt any excess dye will not settle on the silk and stain it. ɔscard the first water and rinse again in clean water. Squeeze ɔt any surplus water, then iron the fixed pieces of silk while ɔey are damp to remove any creases and restore the sheen.

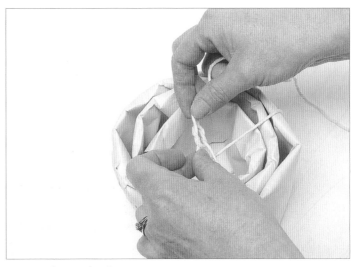

Securing the parcel with string.

Secured parcel sitting on a trivet in the pressure cooker, with a foil "hat."

Pressure cooker on a cooker ring ready for steaming.

STEAM-FIXING IN A BAMBOO STEAMER OR COLANDER AND SAUCEPAN

Follow the instructions for rolling and coiling up to form the parcel as before. Line a bamboo basket or colander with some absorbent paper, such as wallpaper lining paper, and place the parcel on it. Place a domed aluminum-foil hat on top of the parcel to protect it from condensation droplets, then fit a lid onto the bamboo steamer, or make a lid from aluminum foil, to trap as much of the steam as possible. Place a good quantity of water in the base of a saucepan, but ensure that it does not come up as far as the base of the colander or basket. Turn up the heat to bring the water to the boil, and then reduce it to a simmer, just enough to maintain a good head of steam. Steam the parcel for between one and two hours, depending on the dyes used and the quantity and thickness of silk, but remember to check the level of the water from time to time, topping it up if necessary to ensure that there is plenty of water to create lots of steam. Once the piece has been steamed long enough to set the dyes, the silk must be washed as described earlier. As a guide, around one hour is usually sufficient for up to 10 ft (3 meters), with larger quantities or heavier silks requiring longer.

SIMPLE OPEN-STEAMING PAN FOR SHIBORI WORK

Shibori open-pan steaming.

Shibori is an ancient Japanese form of dyeing involving pleating, folding, twisting, wrapping, or stitching silk using bindings of fine threads or string. Shibori work can be easily

fixed in a microwave or steamed while placed on a rack over some boiling water in a roasting pan on top of the stove. An oblong roasting pan is the right shape to take a tube and can also hold a good quantity of water. The metal cooling rack will support the work above the level of the water, yet easily allow the steam to penetrate around the work. The use of a plastic sink drainer protects the silk from direct contact with the metal rack, which can become quite hot over a long period of steaming, and the aluminum foil is wrapped over the work to form a lid and trap the steam. The timing for steaming work in this way will vary according to the size and thickness of the work being fixed, but will range from 40 minutes to two hours. It is important to check that there is enough water in the pan to create the steam, or else the work can become scorched.

COMMERCIAL SILK-STEAMERS

Designs of commercially available silk-steamers vary considerably. Some are electrical, while others must be placed over a heat source. Most are cylindrical or rectangular in shape, allowing the silk to be rolled in absorbent paper, frequently on a pole, which is then suspended either vertically or horizontally above the water source and gently steamed for several hours. Again, times vary considerably according to the model, amount and type of silk being fixed, so refer to the manufacturer's instructions for further guidance.

WHICH STEAMING METHOD IS BEST?

The advantage of commercially available steamers is that you do not have to coil up the paper roll containing the silk piece, therefore reducing the potential of creasing. The disadvantage is the initial cost as they are rather expensive and, depending on the size, can take up quite a lot of floor space, so they may only be a consideration for the serious silk painter or possibly a school or college.

The results from the pressure cooker and bamboo steamer are the same as from a commercial steamer, with the advantage that pressure cooking is the fastest method. As many people now use a microwave for fast cooking, you will probably be able to find a second-hand pressure cooker very cheaply if you do not already have one.

The advantage of using a bamboo steamer to fix the silk dye is that although the process takes longer, bamboo steamers are both very cheap andavailable in a range of sizes, so it is a very inexpensive way of fixing your silk paintings.

IQUID FIXATIVES

ome steam-fix silk dyes can also be set by applying a liquid
xative solution directly onto the finished, dry design as an
ternative fixing method. The precise application can vary
ightly, so do check the manufacturer's instructions before
roceeding. One way of applying the fixative solution is to
ompletely immerse the dry, finished piece in a bath of fixative
lution, agitate for the correct amount of time, and then rinse
e silk in cool water to remove the excess solution, together
ith any loose dye or salt deposits.

Other liquid fixatives require the solution to be brushed over
e entire piece of work while it is still on the frame, then left
r around one hour before washing it off, along with any
rplus dye, water-soluble outliner, and excess salt deposits. Any
xative solution tends to soften the colors slightly, which does
ot necessarily make it a less effective fixing process, merely an
ternative. It can be very effective to work a background and
quid-fix it to achieve a softer look, then rework the silk with
overlaid pattern, this time using a steam-fixing process to
ve a much more vibrant and contrasting color strength. Since
e initial colors are already fixed, they will stay in the original
rmation and will not be affected when the second design is
yered on top. Liquid-fixing can also be used if the finished
lors appear too bright once worked, and a softer appearance
ould be preferable for that particular piece. Not all dyes can be
quid-fixed, however, so check the manufacturer's instructions
r their suitability.

Outliners and Resists

One of the main ways of controlling the spread of silk paints or
dyes is to use a resist line as a barrier to contain the color
within a particular area. These barrier lines can be worked in a
variety of resist mediums: an acrylic heat-fix outliner; a water-
soluble outliner; gutta, a latex medium the consistency of
honey; or a wax resist. The resist line defines the pattern and is
usually drawn directly from a tube or fine nozzle fitted on a soft,
plastic pipette bottle. Although it is not essential, a fine metal
tip can be fitted onto the bottle nozzle to give finer control for
the formation of a resist line.

The resist medium must penetrate through the stretched silk
to seal the fibers on the top and lower surfaces of the silk in
order to form an effective barrier line. There is no set line
thickness to aim for, but the resist line should be in proportion
to the design, pleasing to the artist, and functional in strength
as a barrier line. As a hand-drawn line, it is inevitable that the
line thickness will vary, although it should not appear clumsy.
The choice of color can significantly affect the finished
appearance of the silk painting, so choose outliner colors with
as much care as when selecting the dyes and paints. Resist lines
are normally traced onto the silk following a paper pattern
placed under the fabric, or drawn freehand directly on to the
silk. With practice, it will be possible to control the thickness of
the barrier line, so do not despair if your lines are not as you
would wish to start with. Practice improving your outlining
skills by following the exercises on pages 46–47, and by working
with a clear outliner as described in the project on page 52.

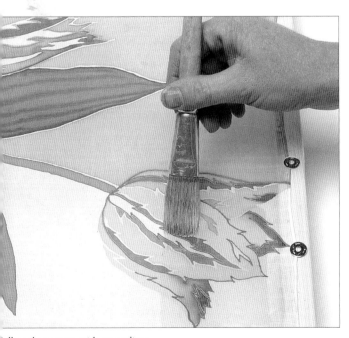

ollow the pattern with an outliner.

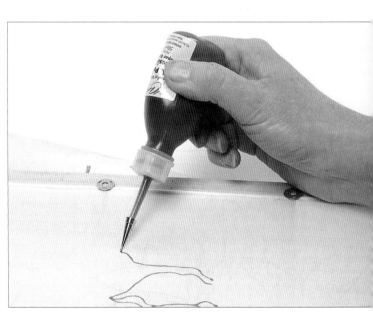

Stenter claw-fitting on a frame.

19

WATER-SOLUBLE AND ACRYLIC OUTLINERS

Water-soluble and acrylic outliners are available in a selection of different colors. They can be clear, matt, or pearlized. The actual outliner medium in both the water-soluble clear and colored matt outliner is designed to wash out after the appropriate fixing method. Pearlized acrylic outliners are intended to remain in the fabric in order to give a pearlized effect and therefore give a very slightly raised, or textured, feel to the silk. A clear or colorless outliner has no pigment, so will give a white line if applied to a white silk, and will always wash completely out of the silk, leaving no trace of stiffness. However, a clear outliner can also be used to give colored or multicolored lines as it will take on the base color of the fabric it is drawn onto: if applied to blue silk, it will give a blue resist line. You can buy ready-colored matt, water-soluble outliners, or make your own by adding a small quantity of dye to clear outliner.

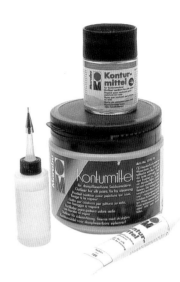

Clear water-based outliners.

A water-soluble outliner will be colored by any paint or dye that is deliberately or accidentally brushed over it and can lose some of its effectiveness as a barrier line if it is subjected to prolonged wetness from either color or water. As it is receptive to color, you can deliberately paint over a water-soluble outliner to disguise a rather chunky line or color it to reduce the impact of the line. Water-soluble outliners are available in both heat-fix and steam-fix types, and are at their strongest as a resist line when dry, which can take around 20–30 minutes, depending on the outline thickness. Speed up the drying time by using a hairdryer, not a heat tool, which can easily scorch the silk. Keep the hairdryer moving to avoid overheating, which may result in fine bubbling in acrylic, pearlized heat-fix outliners. Paint or dye should always be applied a little distance away from the dry line and allowed to run up to the resist line. This will prevent you accidentally painting over the line.

GUTTA PERCHA AND SOLVENT-BASED RESISTS

Gutta percha, usually referred to as gutta, comes from a milky latex substance collected from a tropical tree. It is processed and refined to form a resist medium that is rubbery, pliable, and water resistant. There are also solvent-based resists with the same qualities.

Gutta gives a resist line that can be painted over without the dye coloring the line as it repels color in a the same way as a wax resist. This is useful when working-in a series of washes, or for very intricate designs where it is difficult accurately to apply the color without accidentally brushing over the resist line.

Gutta is quite sensitive to temperature and should not be subjected to extremes of temperature. It should flow like runny honey, but may require thinning with special thinners or a few drops of white spirit to achieve a working consistency as it can thicken during storage. To prevent thickening, keep the pipette bottles in a screw-top jar that contains a little white spirit for a day or two. Any unused gutta should be poured back into the original container because if left to air-dry in the pipette bottles it will harden and become unusable. Solvent-based gutta is most frequently available in clear and black, but you can color your own by adding a little steam-fix dye to clear gutta. Once applied to the silk, it takes about 15–20 minutes to air-dry, although solvent-based gutta forms an effective barrier to the flow of silk dye even before it is completely dry. Solvent-based gutta lines will not wash out in water after the fixing process and must be removed from the finished piece by immersing the silk in white spirit or by dry cleaning. Care must always be taken when using solvent-based products. The solvents used in gutta are flammable and should not be inhaled. Always use and store solvent-based gutta away from any heat source and work in a well-ventilated area. If you do not like working with solvent-based gutta because of the smell and safety factors, substitute a wax resist for a similar working style.

WAX RESIST

Wax gives an excellent water-resistant line that preserves the color of the silk under the waxed area even if dye color is brushed over the top. Wax can be applied by brush, sponge, a canting or tjanting tool, woodcut blocks, or other blocking or printing tools. When applied to silk, wax should look almost transparent. If it looks white or milky, it is too cool and has not penetrated the silk, so that the dyes may be able to creep under the wax. Wax can be removed from silk on completion of a painting by ironing the work between sheets of absorbent paper, such as old newsprint or wallpaper lining paper. Ironing will also set the silk-paint colors at the same time if heat-fix colors have been used. If steam-fix dyes have been used to color the work, the work should first be ironed to remove most of the wax, then steamed as normal to set the dyes. The steaming will also help to remove any last traces of wax.

SAFETY POINTS WHEN USING WAX

- Wax should be heated in a thermostatically controlled wax pot, or a double saucepan with a thermometer to prevent overheating, to a working temperature of 250°F/130°C.

- If the wax smokes, it is too hot; lower the heat source and avoid inhaling the smoke.

- Should the wax ignite, smother the flames with a heat-proof lid or fire blanket. Turn off the heat source and leave the wax pot to cool down. Do not pick it up and try to move it. Never use water to extinguish the flames.

- Never leave a wax pot unattended while it is in use.

Solvent gutta and its storage in a jar.

Basic Techniques of Silk Painting

Tensioning Silk

Most silk painting is worked with the silk fabric stretched on to a frame and held with silk pins. The simplest are small, three-pointed silk pins, which push into the soft, wooden-frame sides.

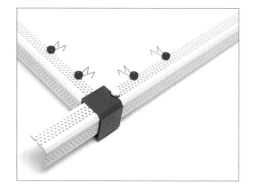

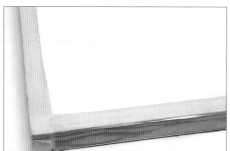

1. Select or set the frame to the correct working size, slightly larger than the piece of silk or to fit a ready-edged scarf. If you are working from a length of fabric, the silk that lies on the frame will not form part of the finished piece. You can cover the wooden frame with tape to help prevent the dyes from marking the frame or new pieces of work.

2. Secure one corner with a silk pin. Hold the silk firmly and pull it taut along one length, then place further pins along this tensioned edge at approximately 2 in. (5 cm) interval

3. Repeat this procedure working along the adjacent edge of the secured corner. Always work away from a fixed point as you will achieve much better tension.

4. On the third edge, you will need to tension both across and down the fabric (weft and warp directions) to remove any looseness on the diagonal. Place pins opposite those already in position as this helps to keep the fabric square.

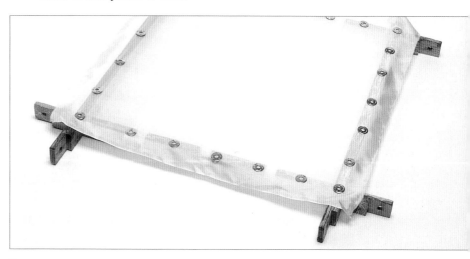

5. Tensioning the fourth side should achieve a tight and even working tension. If you run your finger across the surface, you will be able to feel ridges where the pins are holding the silk. Try to avoid any floppy areas where the silk is too loose, or hard, shiny ridges where the silk is too tight. Adjust and reposition pins as necessary to achieve the correct working tension.

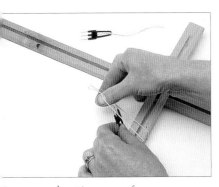

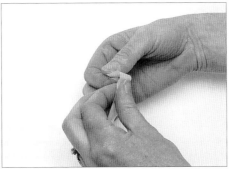

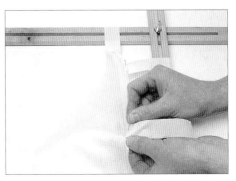

...ing stenter claw pins on to a frame.   *Folding tape to make your own claw pins.*   *Attaching tape with a pin at the edge of the silk.*

...ENTER, OR CLAW, PINS

...enter, or claw, pins are an alternative to three-pointed pins and ... very useful when working with ready-edged pieces or ...kward-sized pieces that will not fit your frame. If you are ...orking with stenter pins, the frame will need to be set out larger ...an the silk to accommodate the length of the pin and the ...etch of the elastic that holds the pin onto the frame. I find that ...s better to replace the elastic bands that are supplied with ...ese pins with thin elastic as it does not snap or perish with use. ...You can make your own stenter-type pins with a length of ...asking tape and a sewing pin. Take a length of masking tape

approximately 6 in. (15 cm) long and fold one end back onto itself. Secure this end to the edge of the silk with a sewing pin. Stretch the length of masking tape out, toward the frame, and stick the tape onto the frame to tension the silk. Repeat this pinning-out at approximately 3 in. (8 cm) intervals around the piece of silk, or along any edges as necessary to achieve a working tension.

If you are working with a frame that comes with its own pins, refer to the manufacturer's instructions.

...OUBLE-SIDED TAPE

...nother way of fastening the silk onto the frame is with double-sided tape. Although this achieves a good tension and makes it easy ... reposition the fabric, it should only be used when working with pieces of silk cut from a length because the strength of the tape can ...ghtly misalign the warp and weft threads as the silk is removed from the frame.

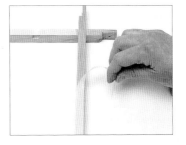

. Set out the frame to the correct working size for the project. Take a reel of double-sided tape and secure the end at one corner of the frame.

2. Run the reel of tape along the whole length of the first side, pressing it firmly into position. Cut the tape and repeat along the other three sides.

3. To position the silk, peel back one length of the backing strip and fasten down the silk, initially in one corner only. Holding the silk taut, line up the edge with the edge of the frame, then gently run a finger along the silk to secure it to the sticky tape.

4. Peel back another backing strip and repeat this process, tensioning the silk before it is stuck to the sticky tape. If the silk is only lightly pressed onto the tape, it can be lifted off and retensioned if necessary without removing the tape from the frame. This will allow the sticky tape to be reused for tensioning further pieces.

Drawing Outlines

Forming an outline, or "resist," to define the pattern and create a barrier, from a resist medium is fundamental to the art of silk painting. The "resist" forms a wall that limits the flow of paint or dye to one particular area of the pattern. Achieving neat resist lines is probably one of the hardest skills to perfect. This section suggests several different ways of applying resist mediums to help you to achieve both effective and esthetically pleasing outlines.

HOW TO APPLY GUTTA, WATER-SOLUBLE, AND ACRYLIC RESIST LINES

If you are drawing out your own design, use a dark-colored, medium-tip, permanent-marker pen to draw the pattern onto the paper. A permanent-marker pen will not smudge or mark the silk if the pattern becomes wet through contact with any of the dyes or water, and a dark pen color is easier to see through the heavier weights of silk. Ideally, use tracing paper so that you can turn the pattern over to work a reversed image, although photocopied patterns also work very well.

Place the tracing-paper pattern under the frame, resting the pattern on some folded newspapers to bring it closer to the underside of the silk. Try to ensure that the taut silk does not make contact with the pattern. Only apply resist to dry silk. Select an outliner color and hold the tube or pipette applicator bottle at approximately 45°, in the way you would hold a pen. Have a piece of kitchen paper handy quickly to wipe the nozzle free of blobs before starting. Place the applicator nozzle down into contact with the silk, look through the silk to the pattern line and gently squeeze the tube or bottle to draw out a resist line. Watch the resist line as it is drawn out so that you can immediately adjust and correct it as it is formed.

It is much easier to adjust the resist line as you draw than to have to redraw a line because it is difficult to match the lines and not get a blob at the joining points. A resist line that is too fine and has not penetrated the top and underside of the silk to form an effective barrier line may allow color to seep through. A line that has been drawn out too quickly allows the tip of the nozzle to skip across the surface of the silk, resulting in a broken or dotted line that will allow color to flow between the gaps.

Continue to trace out all of the pattern lines, remembering to use more than one color of resist if this benefits the piece, until the design is complete. Allow the lines to dry or use a hairdryer to speed up the drying time. Make sure that you remember to remove the tracing pattern before starting painting so that you do not see a double image, which may be confusing. If possible, start working at the top of the design to help avoid smudging or if there is a border, do this first to help define the outer edges of the piece and prevent color from running onto the frame itself.

If you find it difficult to work without any support for your hand, try forming a fist and resting your drawing arm on it to steady your hand. It is also possible to apply some of the resist lines, allow them to dry, and then work more of the design to avoid smudging larger pieces. Before you start painting, always thoroughly check the outlines for gaps—holding the frame up to the light often exposes any holes in the resist lines.

This is probably the most common way of working when starting out, and even an accomplished silk painter can find it helpful to work out a design on paper before committing outlines to silk. Many of the projects in this book can be worked in this way by photocopying and enlarging the patterns from the back of the book.

TRACING OUT A DESIGN WITH THE AID OF A PENCIL OR WATER-SOLUBLE PEN

If you are working on a thicker weight of silk and cannot see the pattern through it, or just prefer not to use a pattern, draw the design out directly on to the silk with a soft pencil or a water-soluble pen (also known as a disappearing pen). If lightly drawn, a soft 4B pencil line should wash out, and any remaining traces of a water-soluble pen will disappear when the silk is first washed. Some disappearing-pen lines vanish after a period of time, varying from a few hours to a couple of days.

If you are using a water-soluble pen, once the resist has been applied on top and is dry, lightly mist some water over the silk to make any remaining pen lines disappear before you start painting. One disadvantage of a water-soluble pen is that the pen line may act as a partial resist line and stop the paint from flowing right up to the real resist line. This results in small, white, unpainted areas of silk showing in the finished piece.

If you are working on a heavy silk, place the pattern on the table, then turn the frame over so that the silk is in contact with the pattern. Use the water-soluble pen to trace out the whole design, then turn the frame back to the correct side and redraw all of the lines in your chosen barrier medium. Remember that working in this way will reverse any image, so be careful with words and numbers.

WORKING A LINE OF RESIST FREEHAND

Sometimes it is easier just to draw straight onto the silk without using a pattern. This enables great spontaneity and freedom, allowing the design to develop as each resist line is drawn. Always keep the tip of the nozzle of the outliner tube or pipette bottle in contact with the silk, and try using your whole body to help you to draw long, unbroken lines by shifting your body weight from one leg to the other as you draw.

Remember that the thickness of line formed comes from a combination of the speed with which you draw the line and the amount of pressure applied to the tube or bottle. Too much pressure will result in thick, clumsy lines, while too little pressure will produce lines that cannot hold the flow of dye color. Blobs form very easily at the end of the applicator nozzle, and also at the start and finish point or the sharp turn of a resist line. With practice, you will be able to control this blobbing more effectively, but there are no shortcuts to good resist lines. Just as with any other skill, the answer is practice, practice, and more practice. Bear in mind that your resist lines are hand-drawn, and that the appearance of a hand-drawn image has an appeal and special quality of its own. Very little in life is completely perfect, so take comfort from this as you work.

Form a fist to support your hand as you outline.

SEQUENTIAL OUTLINING WITH A CLEAR RESIST

You can create some very interesting designs using a resist line both to define the pattern and control the spread of the dyes, but in such a way that the line is less obvious, which results in a softer, less stenciled appearance.

Lay down an initial background of dye color, allow this to dry, and draw the clear resist line onto this colored ground. Then add further dye to rework some areas of the design and allow this second layer of color to dry. Continue to work in this way, drawing out resist lines, allowing them to dry, and applying further color. This gives the finished work a layered effect where the resist lines have less impact on the design, yet the use of resist has allowed full control over the spread of color at the working stage. When applying a series of resist lines followed by reworking in this way, it is possible to apply the subsequent dye to any part of the design to enhance and strengthen the color or shapes formed. It is easier to use steam-fix dyes when working in this way as heat-fix paints do not flow so readily after the second layer of color.

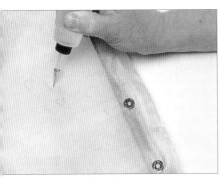

Sequential outlining: first draw out clear outlines.

Repainting the background in a sequential-outlining piece.

A shot of the finished sequential-outlining effect.

USING CLEAR RESIST AS AN INVISIBLE BARRIER LINE

Using clear resist as an invisible barrier.

As well as working in a series of layers to minimize the impact of a resist line, it is possible to work in such a way that the resist line does not show at all. Since all colorless resist mediums, whether gutta, water-soluble outliner, or wax, can be completely removed from the silk, you can use the advantages of working in a controlled way, but remove the evidence of their presence in the finished piece.

The resist line used for this technique must be colorless, but can be applied to plain white or colored silk. Once the resist lines have been drawn onto the silk, the silk paint or dye must only be applied up to *either* the inner or outer edge of the resist lines throughout the whole piece. Once the work has been fixed in the appropriate way and the resist lines removed, there will be no evidence of a barrier line around the shape. A resist or barrier line will only show on the finished work if color is applied up to both edges of the resist line.

If a design is drawn in clear resist on white silk and painted leaving the background white, the lines will disappear completely after the work is fixed and the resist lines removed. The design motifs will appear on a white background without the apparent evidence of use of resist. This way of working can also be applied to colored silk, as long as the silk dye or paint is only applied to one edge of the resist lines. Please refer to the projects on pages 52 and 79 for working in this way.

RULING STRAIGHT LINES FOR BORDERS AND GEOMETRIC DESIGNS

Although it is possible to work a reasonably straight line freehand with a little practice, a straight line for borders or geometric designs can easily be achieved. Find a couple of pieces of wood that are slightly higher than the height of the silk-painting frame, place them on each side, and rest a long ruler like a meter rule or yard stick on them to form a bridge. Hold the rule in position, ensuring that your fingers will not be in the way as you draw out the line by running the applicator nozzle along the edge of the rule. The spacing of the lines can be done by eye, or by marking set points along the edges of the frame or silk using a plastic canvas grid with a water-soluble marker pen.

Use a plastic-canvas square grid to mark out border widths and corner points. (See the Materials and Equipment section on page 12 for instructions on how to make a grid from plastic canvas.) Place the plastic-canvas square grid into each corner in turn, marking out the corner points with a water-soluble pen or soft pencil in the appropriate hole on the grid. Then use the support to make a bridge and line up the rule to join up the corner marks and form an even border without lots of measuring out.

Making a bridge.

Marking out corner points with a plastic-canvas square grid.

Joining up corner points using a ruler to draw out a resist line.

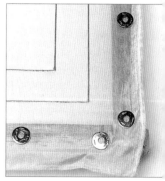

The finished, marked-out corner.

Silk-paint Thickeners

Silk paints and dyes can be mixed with a thickener medium, which takes away the normal, free-flowing properties of a liquid color and creates a medium that can be used as an alternative resist or paint medium. Silk-paint thickeners are clear or honey-colored gelatinous substances. They should be added in roughly equal quantities, proportionate to the dye, and thoroughly mixed to combine the two elements into a colored medium. For a colorless resist, apply the thickener directly to the silk without the addition of any color.

Before applying any color to the silk, allow the thickener to dry or use a hairdryer. Apply the colors in the normal way, placing the brush a little distance away from the thickener lines or motifs, and allow the colors to flow across the silk up to the thickener. The paints and dyes will stop at the areas where thickener has been applied in the same way that color stops at a resist line. Once the painting is completed and fixed in the appropriate way, the silk should be washed to remove the dried thickener medium, which slightly stiffens the fabric at the working stage. Once washed, it should retain the usual degree of softness and drape expected from the silk paints or dyes used to color the piece.

Paint thickeners can be applied by brush, sponge, or print blocks to create either a pattern with a linear design or patterned shapes of resistance. Since the application of thickener in these ways does not require the same fine hand control, it can be particularly useful for people with stiffness of the hand or arthritis, or anyone without good hand coordination skills. If using a water-soluble thickener, remember that any color sprayed or brushed over the dry thickener will penetrate through the medium and slightly color the silk.

The use of thickened silk paint gives a softer, less stenciled appearance to the finished piece and allows the transition of one color into another without a fine resist line separating the two. The strength of the barrier quality of the thickener medium can be adjusted by varying the amount of thickener applied to the silk or by slightly adjusting the proportionate mix. To form a definite edge to the pattern, apply a generous amount of thickener medium or create a much softer barrier by applying less thickener medium to the silk. A slightly higher proportion of dye to thickener will create a looser, weaker resist, which will also allow some deliberate spreading of the color across the thickener.

It is possible to combine the use of resist lines and thickener within the same piece to add further interest to the work. If you use both, do not apply gutta or outliner over the top of the thickener because it will not be able to bond with the silk and will become detached at the washing stage when the thickener is rinsed away. (See projects on pages 64 and 87.)

Thickener sponges, stamps, color, and thickener.

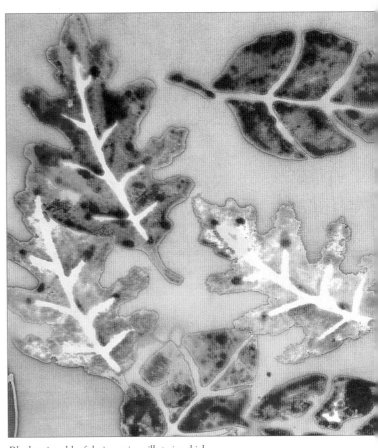

Block-printed leaf design using silk-paint thickener.

Applying Color

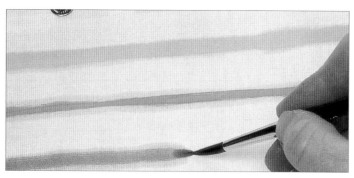

Striping down color.

Silk paints and dyes offer a fascinating way of working because of their wonderful, free-flowing qualities. Brushes are an excellent tool for lifting and applying color, and can also release color in a controlled way. Try working a striped pattern by forming stripes of equal thickness. It is possible to achieve this just by using the tip of the brush initially, and then, as the stripe is brushed out, pressing the brush down to give greater contact with the silk. Further stripes can be added to form overlapping or tartan patterns, with blended or watermarked edges, depending on whether the additional stripes are added to wet or dry silk and by varying the spreading gap.

Rinse your brushes in a large water pot and always use a piece of kitchen towel to dry them after rinsing. This ensures that the colors remain at the correct strength, untainted or diluted.

Always allow the color to flow toward an outline rather than putting it down next to an outline. This spreading distance ensures that the outlines are not swamped with color and prevents the tide of color from flowing across, or under, a weak resist line. It also gives you time to repair any gaps before too much color has escaped.

The best position for placing color on an outlined shape will vary depending on the size, complexity, and coloring effect of the shape to be filled. As a general rule, place the color in the center of simple, medium-sized shapes, so that the color flows evenly to the outer edges. For complex, long, thin, or very large shapes, it may be better to place the color at one end and allow it to move along the shape like a tide flowing up a river estuary, gradually filling all the nooks and crannies as it progresses.

Gridding on tartan stripes.

COLORING A DAISY

Take the shape of a daisy as an example to illustrate various color-placement positions.

One area of one color: if the daisy is small- to medium-sized and formed from one outlined shape that is to be one color, the color should be applied from the brush as a central reservoir in the center of the daisy. The dry silk will absorb the color and allow it to flow up into each of the petals. By estimating the amount of paint or dye required to color the whole shape, it can be colored by one application of paint or dye. However, if more is required, use the brush to reapply a small, further quantity of color to complete the shape. Observe how the silk absorbs the color and wait until all of the dye has been absorbed before adding any more if you think it necessary. If puddles of color remain on the surface of the silk once the shape has been completely painted in, you are applying too much. Remove any excess color with a dry brush or cotton bud to prevent it from seeping across any weak barrier lines.

Apply color to the center of a shape.

Removing excess color with a cotton bud.

several shapes of one color: if the daisy shape is formed from a ground center with separate petals, which are to be the same color, each petal should be painted individually by placing the color in the center of each petal and completing it before moving on to the next one. By following this rule, you will be able to concentrate properly on just one segment of the whole shape rather than trying to paint several petal shapes at once. This method of working is of particular benefit with large or complex shapes. Once all of the petals have been painted, the center shape can also be colored.

Complete each petal shape before moving on to the next one.

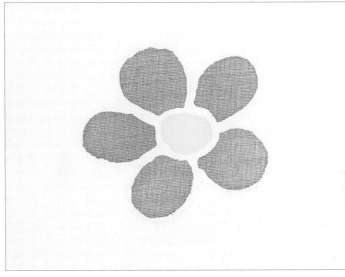

The completed daisy, with the center area painted in last.

Shapes with one color blended at different strengths: blending color from full strength to a lighter, more diluted color adds depth and reality to a design. First apply a little water to the area of the petal that you wish to remain pale, near the center, for example. This acts as a stop and prevents the darker color from swamping the whole shape. Then use a small brush to work one petal at a time and apply a tiny quantity of the deeper-strength color at the tip of the petal. Quickly rinse and dry the brush with kitchen paper, then lift up a little mid-strength color and apply this with an overlapping brushstroke. Repeat this process with a lighter tint until you can blend into the water. Use a clean brush to blend each tint of color into the next to achieve a gradual shading effect. Repeat this process with each petal in turn until the flower is complete, then go back and paint the center of the daisy. This technique for shading can be applied to any shape or size of shape by adjusting the brush sizes and varying the number of tints to fit the area of the shape being worked.

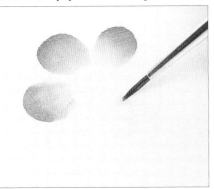

Applying the lightest color.

Brushing in the mid-strength color.

Blending in the darkest color.

One shape halo-shaded with color at different tonal strengths: water will flow across silk in the same way as colors, so water can be used to create shading. First, place some color in the center of the daisy shape and allow it to flow out to the outline edge; then, before the first color has completely dried on the silk, add a small quantity of water to the center of the shape. The water will push some of the first color outward, concentrating the color at the outline edge and giving a shaded-halo effect. This effect can also be worked by using another color to displace the initial color.

Creating a halo shading with water.

One large, outlined shape: if the shape to be colored is too large to apply color from the center, allowing it to spread outward, it is more effective to apply the color to the tip of one petal and work the color toward the center. At the center, introduce color into the two adjoining petals, keeping the center spreading edge wet, and gradually move on to the next petals until the whole flower is painted in. It is possible to have both fast-track and slow-track leading or spreading edges. As long as you keep a leading edge wet with small top-ups of color, you can concentrate on other areas without a hard watermark forming. Try to paint in one p[art] of the shape completely before moving on to the next part. Th[is] avoids having to go back to an almost dry or dry area with further color, which will cause a watermark where the wet col[or] displaces the damp color.

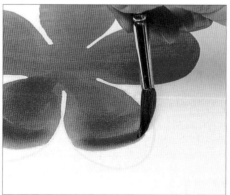

1. *Start applying the color at the edge of the shape.*

2. *Completely paint this area.*

3. *Start to introduce color to the adjoining area.*

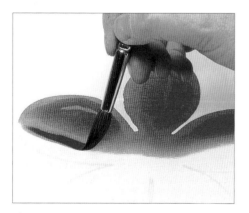

4. *Use bold strokes to keep the spreading edge wet.*

5. *If necessary, have several spreading edges and keep them moving by working them alternately.*

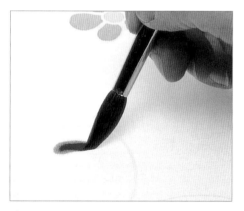

6. *The completed shape, with even coloring an[d] no watermarks.*

Repairing Color Leaks Through a Resist Line

Sometimes color can seep through a resist line even though there is no obvious gap. If this happens, you can reduce the impact of the escaped color to a minimum, and sometimes to a point where it will not be noticeable at all. There may be a slight change in the flow of color across the silk in areas where you have lifted up escaped color. Slight marks or a reluctance of flow can usually be overcome by rubbing the fabric with a brush to encourage the color to penetrate the silk.

COLOR SEEPING THROUGH A RESIST LINE

Color can break through a resist line for the following reasons.

- The resist line was too fine, or not dense or strong enough, to form a barrier.
- The resist did not properly penetrate the silk, allowing the color to seep under the line.
- Too much color was applied too close to the resist line and swamped it.
- The brush accidentally brushed across the resist line, taking the color with it.

Should any of these reasons be the cause of color seepage, the following corrective measures can be worked to improve unwanted coloring on the wrong side of the resist line.

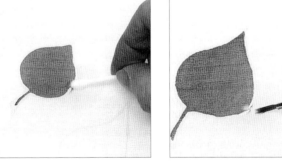

Apply water in an arc around the escaped color.

Lift up the escaped color with a cotton bud.

Repeat the application of water if necessary.

Use a clean cotton bud to dry off the area.

Following the unwanted seepage, quickly rinse your brush in clean water and apply a little water in an arc *around* the escaped color. Do not apply water directly to the color because this will cause the color to spread out even farther. Instead, allow the water to run up to the edge of the seepage and push all of the escaped color back toward the resist line, preventing a hard, watermark edge from forming. While the color is moving back toward the resist line, use a cotton bud to wipe the surface of the silk to lift up the escaped color. Repeat this process carefully, as many times as necessary, to pick up as much color as you can. Be careful not to swamp the area with water because this may cause further problems if the water breaks through an already weak resist line to the inside of the shape. Should this happen, blot the inside area with another cotton bud before repairing the resist line to prevent further seepage.

COLOR ESCAPING THROUGH GAPS IN THE RESIST LINE

As soon as you see color escaping through a gap, blot the area with a cotton bud and then close the gap by reapplying a little resist to seal the break. Then apply a little water in an arc around the escaped color as described before. Any escaped color from heat-set paints must be cleared up before they dry; steam-fix colors can be treated even after they have dried. If steam-fi dyes are being used, it may be easier to lift up the escaped dye the reapplied outliner is first dried. This allows the cotton bud be taken right up to the repaired gap without the risk of smearing the wet outliner.

LIFTING UP SPOTS OF UNWANTED COLOR

It can be very annoying if a spot of color drops from your paintbrush onto the silk. Should this happen, the damage can be minimized by quickly rinsing and drying the brush before lifting up clean water, which is circled around the unwanted spot. The water will spread and concentrate the color spill into a smaller spot, which should then be gently rubbed with a cotton bud to lift up the color. Repeat this circling process with further applications of clean water until the damage is minimized. Slig coloration can normally be covered by the background color o hidden by the addition of a little more outlining. This correcti measure will work effectively on white unpainted silk or on a c completed area if heat-fix paints have been used.

An unwanted spot of color.

Circle clean water around the spot of color.

Use a cotton bud to lift up the unwanted color spill.

Apply more clean water if needed. Reblot with a cotton bud.

Painting in Backgrounds

Successfully painting in large, complex backgrounds, especially if they have lots of shapes to paint around, is one of the hardest things to achieve. Minimize the size and complexity of a background at the design stage by allowing shapes to link together, or incorporate a border to reduce the overall size of the background. Always ensure that you have sufficient color before starting to paint; notice how much is in your palette before starting and then check how much remains once you have completed the background. This allows you to build up an awareness of approximately how much color is required for a particular area.

PAINTING A BACKGROUND AREA OF ONE COLOR

Start in a corner.

Work the color around the shapes.

Keep the edge wet with color to avoid watermarks.

Avoid going back by totally painting in the area.

Finish in an opposite corne

ore you start, check to see where the best starting pointis.
nember the rule of the incoming tide moving up a river
uary, together with the fast- and slow-track methods of
plying color. Once you have decided where to start, work the
or onward, across the work, in a controlled way. Top up color
ng some spreading or leading edges to keep the silk wet, and
-track work on other spreading edges until they are
npletely painted in. When you have completed one area, go
k to the slow-track spreading edges and concentrate on the
t appropriate one. A corner is often a good place to start,
n move down and across, while fanning out and around

shapes, keeping all spreading edges wet, until the whole
background has been painted. Bring your palette closer to the
area you are painting to prevent accidental drips landing on
your work.

Ensure that you have completely painted in behind the spread
of the leading edge, especially in all of the small nooks and
crannies, before progressing onward, to prevent having to go
back to an area that was accidentally missed, which usually
results in a watermark. It is always better to allow a background
to dry naturally because using a hairdryer can cause rings to form
through uneven drying.

ACKGROUND AREAS WITH MORE THAN ONE COLOR

hen painting in a large area or background with several colors
nded together, it is better to start with the lightest color first,
dually working toward the deeper color. It is possible to paint
ckgrounds with the silk dry or predampened, depending on
ir personal preferences and experience. Large areas of silk can
predampened with either water or dilutant, or a mixture of
ohol and water in a 2:1 ratio, to help color-blending and to
vent watermarks from forming.

As the dampness of the silk slows down the flow of the color,
unwanted halo marks can form along the edges of the pattern
lines where the water prevents the color from spreading right up
to the resist line. To reduce this, carefully take the brush right up
to the resist line and check that the dampness is not preventing
the coloring of small, finely detailed shapes.

Wet-into-wet for a Watercolor Effect

REE-FLOW COLOR

ints and dyes flow freely across the silk without interruption
d stop at resist lines. As color reaches the limit of its flow, a
corative edge is formed, which is referred to as a watermark.
atermarks can be incorporated into a design by encouraging
em to form in a particular place. They work particularly well
landscape pictures depicting hills, trees, or implied features,
in floral designs, where their decorative edge can be a
ry effective way of creating the veins of leaves and petals
flowers.
Working in this way can be more difficult than working
thin a set framework provided by resist lines as the design
ies much more on your control of the movement of the dyes.

Steam-fix dyes are the most suitable because the colors can be
applied in a series of layers and moved into new positions,
forming new watermarks each time. A steam-fix color is capable
of movement across the silk and is vulnerable to contact with
water until it has been fixed. Layering the colors and forming
watermarks is still possible with heat-fix colors, but the
patterning must be done while the colors are still damp to
achieve any movement of the paints because a heat-fix color will
not move into new patterns once it has dried. Practice a few
times on a sampler, or try working the project on page 100 that
uses this technique with minimal resist usage.

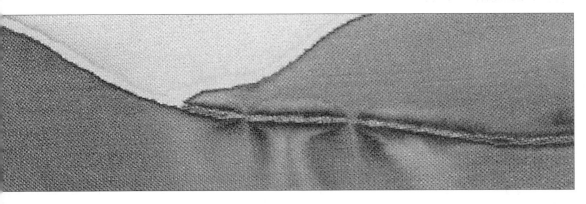

*Free-flow color on a
landscape card*

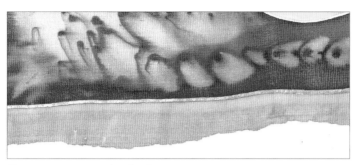

Texture patterns created with salt.

Working With Effect Salt

You can create some beautiful textural patterns using salt granules. Dry salt soaks up the wet silk paint or dye and forms wonderful, frostlike patterns. By using various sizes of salt grain and crystals it is possible to vary the size of the pattern marks. Table salt produces very fine pattern marks, while coarse sea sa dishwasher salt, and commercial effect salt produce larger mar

HOW TO ACHIEVE SALT-EFFECT PATTERNS SUCCESSFULLY

To work this technique, you must place or scatter the salt onto the silk while the paints or dyes are still wet. If the work is too dry the salt cannot absorb the color to form the patterns. You may achieve small, starry patterns but not the impressive, frosty, flowing patterns that are associated with salt. If the work is too wet, the salt may become saturated too quickly and will not pull further patterns until the work has dried a little and the correct balance and optimum conditions are achieved. Impressive patterns develop when all of the salt crystals have a little working space of their own. If the salt is too heavily applied, it produces large, bleached-out areas, with little patterning.

It is best to leave the salt on the silk until it is dry, although you can reposition it while the patterns are still being formed. Never be tempted to use a hairdryer to dry a work with salt still on the silk because this results in a shower of colored salt landing over the whole piece. It is best to use table, sea, and dishwasher salt only once and then to throw it away, although it is possible to recycle commercial, special-effect salts.

Always make sure that any resist lines are completely dry before using salt because it can become stuck in the resist line, possibly damaging it on removal. To prevent salt-effect pattern appearing where you don't want them, make sure that you remove any stray crystals that have jumped onto the wrong patch of silk. If possible, save any salt patterning till last, maki sure that all of the other sections are dry.

Once you have finished, it is vital to remove all of the salt from the work before fixing, especially if you are steam-fixing Salt crystals left on the silk can cause spot marks to appear during the steam-fixing process. You may notice that some of t very dark, freckling marks made when working with salt disappear when the work is washed for the first time. This is ju the base of the salt crystal being removed from the silk rather than the paint or dye washing out. After the appropriate fixing method is complete, the silk should always be washed to remov any traces of salt.

Salt effect on the edge of a drawstring bag.

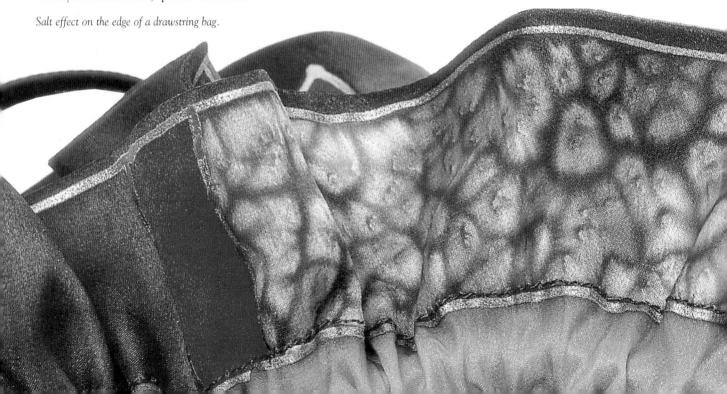

Working With Antifusants, No-flow, or Antispreads

We have already looked at a thickener medium that changes the flow properties of the color, but it is also possible to change the flow properties of the silk. By treating the silk with a liquid antispread, the colors can be applied to it in a controlled way, without the need for a resist.

Antispread solution, which is clear or white in color, is available for both heat- and steam-fix colors, and can be applied to the whole or just part of the silk. Once dry, the silk will behave more like a dry cartridge paper, holding the color where it is placed for fine work, or if the colors are applied as a wet-on-wet technique, they will mix and blend. You can work effectively in layers or from a pattern placed under the silk in the normal way, following the shape of the pattern without applying a resist line, giving the finished work a watercolor appearance.

On completion of the painting, the work should be fixed in the appropriate way and then washed. Antispread solutions can leave a slight trace of stiffness to the silk, so are more suitable for projects where the drape and flow of the silk are of less importance, for example, cards, pictures, banners, and pillow panels. Please refer to the project on page 92 for practice in this technique.

Leaves painted on silk treated with antispread.

Watermark Patterning

As mentioned earlier, it is possible to create watermarks as texture patterning within a design. The most dramatic watermarks are formed when applying further steam-fix dyes, water, alcohol, or diffusing medium to dry areas of painted silk. The second application of dye or liquid pushes aside the first layer of color to create a beautiful, crinkly edge. The effect is softened if the work is still damp when the second or subsequent application of color or liquid is applied, creating lovely, soft rings or pattern lines of a lighter shade. This patterning can overwork and lose the dramatic effect if it is always left to dry naturally, so keep watching the developing pattern and dry it with a hairdryer at the appropriate time. Cotton buds can be used to lift up excess

liquid once the desired effect has formed to control the final result. When using some steam-fix dyes it is more effective to use alcohol or diffusing medium in place of water to create these watermarks.

Because water, alcohol, and diffusing medium all spread across the silk by capillary action, they can also be used to reserve areas as white, unpainted silk. Any of these will act as a stop to the spread of the colors if they are applied to areas of silk that you wish to remain white or very pale before any color is introduced. The joining line where color and medium meet will form a soft, paler line that can be blended together by working over the area with a clean, dry brush.

Watercolor effect.

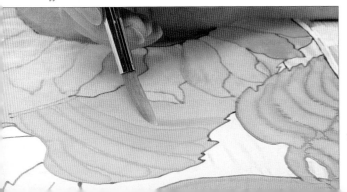

Watercolor effect on a sampler.

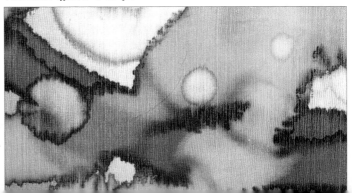

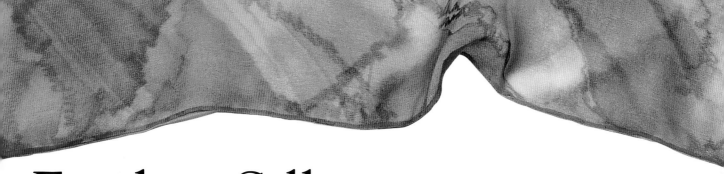

Further Silk-painting Techniques

Working on Velvet

Working on silk velvet is another strand in the silk painter's skills. The velvet most frequently used is a mix of fibers and is made up of silk, a protein fiber for the backing, and viscose, a cellulose fiber for the pile. This combination of fibers allows the use of a fiber-etch gel to work a devorée pattern into the velvet for an additional textural effect. Devorée means "burned out," and involves the removal of the pile by etching out or carbonizing the cellulose-based fiber. The most suitable dyes to color silk-viscose velvet are either steam-fix or procion dyes. Both work well and give excellent depth of color. If steam-fixed dyes are used, follow the steaming instructions given earlier. The advantage of working with a procion dye on velvet is that you do not have to steam the finished design to set the colors.

The fixing process is achieved by a chemical reaction from the use of a soda-ash solution applied either directly to the dyes or as a fixing-bath solution. There are many different recipes for fixing procion dyes, and they often include salt, urea, and soda ash in varying quantities.

Salt helps to dissolve the dye and drive it into the fiber.

Urea is available in granular form and also helps to dissolve the dye and drive it into the fiber.

Soda ash is available as a powder, but when dissolved in water creates an alkaline solution that helps the dye bond to the fiber of the fabric.

Safety Notes

- Care should be taken with procion dyes while they are in the powder state. Avoid inhaling the dye powder and wear a protective mask when measuring out and mixing up these dyes. Rubber gloves should be worn when handling chemicals.

- The dye powder should be added to the water, not the other way around, but once the dyes have been mixed there is no danger of inhalation and therefore it is not necessary to continue to wear the mask.

- Wear a protective mask when tearing silk-viscose fabric as the fine fibers could also be an irritant if inhaled.

- Always label any containers of dyes or chemicals clearly.

Materials and equipment for painting on velvet.

rocion Dyes

ocion dyes are cold-water-reactive dyes that are set with a
la-ash solution. They work on many natural fibers, including
, wool, cotton, linen, paper, and rayon, but are particularly
d with plant fibers, making them ideal for silk-and-viscose-
velvets. Procion dyes are normally available in powder form
d need to be mixed with water to form a liquid dye. Both
ocion dyes and steam-fix dyes can be applied with Chinese-
le paintbrushes or foam brushes, without the need for resists
en working on velvet.

The soda-ash solution needed to set procion dyes can be added
her while mixing up the dye, and be applied as the dyes are
painted onto the fabric, or else applied as a fixative bath after
the dyes have been poured onto the silk velvet. However, once
the soda-ash solution has been added to the dyes, it starts the
chemical reaction that bonds the dyes with the fibers, with an
effective working time of approximately three hours.

These dyes can be applied with a brush to work a defined and
controlled design, by dipping the silk velvet into a large
container, or by adding several colors to a dyeing bucket or tray
for random and blended colors. Use the following steps to work
the dyeing process in a dye bath or tray.

YEING SILK-VISCOSE VELVET IN A BUCKET OR TRAY

ld ¹/₂ pint (250 ml) of boiling water to two tablespoons of
dinary table salt in a heat-proof measuring jug. Stir well until
e salt has dissolved and then add cold water to make up to 1
nt (500 ml). Wearing a protective mask, measure out ¹/₂
aspoon of procion-dye powder (more if you want a stronger
lor) and add this to a jam jar with ¹/₄ pint (125 ml) of the salt-
ater solution. Stir well to dissolve the procion powder and then
p up this colored-dye solution with a further ¹/₄ pint (125 ml)
cold water. Increase these quantities proportionately for
eater quantities of dye. Have a standard teaspoon measure,
nether flat or heaped, to allow for a greater degree of
nsistency when remixing to achieve a similar strength of color
nen working with powdered dyes.

Wet the velvet with water, then gently squeeze out the excess
and arrange the fabric randomly, or into a semistructured
pattern, in the base of the bucket or tray. Prewetting the silk
helps to achieve a more even coloring. Carefully pour the liquid
dye onto the fabric and gently agitate the tray, or wear rubber
gloves and mix the colors with your hands. The more you handle
the fabric, the more blended and muted the colors become. If the
velvet is sitting in large quantities of dye, pour this away and
then leave the velvet to rest for at least 20 minutes, preferably
longer. The velvet can be left for several hours to maximize the
uptake and blending of colors.

IXING UP THE FIXATIVE SOLUTION FOR DYEING IN A BATH OR TRAY

fixative solution of soda ash must be added to the dye bath to
the dyes. Dissolve one tablespoon of soda ash in ¹/₂ pint (250
) of boiling water and stir to dissolve, then add a further ¹/₂
nt (250 ml) of cold water. Remove any dye liquid left in the
e bath, then pour the soda-ash fixing solution over the dyed
lvet. Slightly agitate the tray to ensure that the fixing solution
s penetrated all areas and leave to cure for at least one hour.

Tip away the fixing solution and rinse out the silk velvet in
ld water. Keep rinsing until the water runs clear. It may take
veral rinses before all the loose dye is removed; try using a little
nthrapol, a liquid detergent that helps to remove excess dye.
Lay out the dyed silk velvet on some old newspaper to dry off
little and then iron on the reverse side while it is still just
mp for a smooth, plush finish.

You can continue working and developing the fabric by adding
vorée patterning or surface decoration for further textural
hancement to the dyed silk velvet. The devorée process is
plained on page 39.

*Measuring out soda-
ash fixative.*

PAINTING A DESIGN ONTO SILK-VISCOSE VELVET WITH PROCION DYES

Measuring out dye and fixative in a jar.

Beautiful designs can be painted on velvet without the need for a barrier as the thickness and absorbency of the fabric allows for only minimal flow of the dyes and fine control over the pattern can be achieved. Adding the soda-ash fixative solution to the dyes in the mixing palette starts the chemical reaction and means that the dyes must be used well within three hours to allow sufficient time for the fixing to work.

Before you begin mixing up the procion dyes for painting onto silk velvet, put on a face mask. Measure out one teaspoon of dye powder and add it to a little hot, but not boiling, water in a measuring jug. Stir to dissolve the dye. Then add cold water to make it up to ¹/₃ pint (200 ml). Pour the dissolved dye into a labeled screw-top jar, where it will keep for several weeks; however, it is better to mix up only the quantity that you need for each project.

Wear rubber gloves to make the fixative solution and measure out and dissolve eight teaspoons of urea granules in ³/₄ pint (400 ml) of hot, but not boiling, water and stir until dissolved. Urea helps the dye powder to dissolve and spread evenly across the silk fabric. Pour this solution into a large, clearly labeled screw-top jar.

Clean out the jug, measure out ten teaspoons of soda ash, dissolve it in ³/₄ pint (400 ml) of hot, but not boiling, water, and stir until the soda ash has dissolved. Each of these two solutions can be made up in advance of your painting and stored in separate, clearly labeled jars. Once again, only make up enough for the project and keep the bulk of your ingredients in their dry form. To prepare an active fixative solution for painting with procion dyes, measure out equal quantities of the prepared urea and soda-ash solutions into a third, clearly labeled, large jar. This combined urea/soda ash forms the fixative solution.

Painting With the Combined Dye and Fixative Solution on Silk-viscose Velvet

Using a plastic pipette dropper, put equal quantities of the prepared procion dye and combined fixative solution in a mixing palette. Once the dye and fixative solution are combined, they will only be viable for three hours and must therefore be applied to the fabric within this time to give the soda ash sufficient time to bond the dye onto the velvet fibers. Combining the fixative and dye in the palette allows working without the need for any further fixing process. The color strength can be adjusted by diluting with water to the required shade and then adding a little more fixative.

Silk velvet does not need to be stretched on a frame. Lay it on some polythene, pile side down, using masking tape to hold it in place. If you prefer to use a frame, pin out the fabric as normal, using either stenter claws or silk pins, but remember to have the fabric pile side down.

Velvet absorbs a lot of dye, which can be applied with Chinese or foam brushes. The dye should always be applied to the reverse of the fabric as this helps it to penetrate the pile and prevents the pattern from spreading too far. The color will spread a little, but a defined pattern can be achieved by controlling the amount of color released by varying the amount of brush contact with the velvet. The tip of a brush will only release a little color, whereas pressing down will release greater quantities of dye. The correct-sized brush in combination with good brush control allows detailed patterns to be achieved without resists.

Once the velvet has been completely painted with the activated dye solution, allow it to air-dry on old newspapers for several hours. It is possible to leave it overnight, but no longer because soda ash forms a strong alkaline solution, which, if left for too long, could damage the silk fibers.

After leaving the velvet for at least three hours, rinse out in cool water to remove any excess dye and spent fixative solution. It will take several rinses before the water runs clear. Gently squeeze out any excess water and allow the fabric to dry on clean, old newspaper. Do not hang the piece on a washing line to dry as any remaining loose dye could run down the fabric and spoil it. When the silk is still just damp, iron the velvet on the wrong side to restore the plush pile finish.

It is now possible to add devorée using a fiber-etch gel, or to employ surface-decoration techniques for further textural effects.

Using Fiber-etch Gel to Create Devorée Patterns

Devorée is the term given to patterns formed by a chemical etching gel that is applied to a protein-and-cellulose mixed-fiber fabric. The fiber-etch gel is usually aluminum sulfate or sodium hydrogen sulfate, which carbonizes the cellulose fiber when heat is applied, creating the etched pattern. Use sodium bicarbonate to neutralize the etching process should the fiber-etch gel accidentally be applied in the wrong position. Fiber-etch gel will work on cotton, linen, viscose, and rayon, which are all cellulose or plant-based fibers. If correctly applied, it should not remove protein-based fibers, such as silk or wool.

Always apply the fiber-etch gel to the wrong side or backing of the silk-viscose velvet. The gel is then applied at the base of the pile to ensure an effective release once the heat has been applied. Fiber-etch gel can be applied to white velvet before any color has been applied, or after the velvet has been painted or dyed. Fiber-etch gel can either be screen-printed or applied direct from the applicator bottle, in a similar way to outliner. The

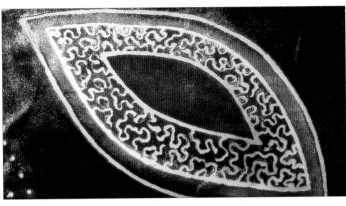

Detail of velvet devorée on a scarf.

screen can be made using a photo-stencil emulsion, or with a stencil fastened to the back of a blank screen with masking tape. Pieces of masking tape stuck to the back of a blank screen can also create a very effective design that can be repeated.

HOW TO APPLY FIBER-ETCH GEL

Work in a well-ventilated room. Cover the work surface with some plastic sheeting and lay the piece of silk velvet pile side down. Tension and hold it in place with masking tape. Use a frame if you prefer.

Wearing a mask and rubber gloves, apply the fiber-etch gel as evenly as you can to the silk backing. Try to avoid any large blobs or areas where the gel is applied too heavily as too much or an uneven amount of fiber-etch gel can potentially create holes when the gel is activated by ironing. If you have large blobs, lift off the excess or distribute it across the area on which you are working. If you are applying the fiber-etch gel direct from the nozzle of the applicator bottle, remember to use light pressure. For screen-printing, eight pulls of the squeegee across the mesh is usually sufficient to achieve a sharp image, with the velvet stretched on the work surface. Work a sampler on a small test piece before starting on a major project if you have not worked this process before.

Once applied to the velvet, the fiber-etch gel should be dried with a hairdryer rather than letting it dry naturally. When dry, iron on the reverse of the velvet, with the iron at silk/wool setting, until the lines become pale brown, taking care not to overheat the work so that it becomes dark brown. The fiber-etch gel is colorless when dry, but the dry heat causes a chemical reaction that carbonizes the cellulose fibers or treated pile of the velvet. The pale-brown color shows that the cellulose fibers have carbonized, not that the fabric is scorched, and will disappear when the fabric is washed. If you cannot easily see this color

change on painted velvet, turn to the pile side of the velvet from time to time to see whether the viscose pile in the treated areas will detach easily from the silk backing when gently rubbed with a finger.

When the whole piece of velvet has been ironed sufficiently, wash it in cool water, gently agitating the velvet to remove the pile and reveal the devorée pattern. Do not detach the pile by shaking or rubbing the velvet when it is dry as this releases the pile fibers into the air, which can cause irritation if inhaled. The fabric is quite fragile at this stage, and rubbing the silk can cause holes to develop. Once the velvet has been rinsed through and the pattern is fully revealed, gently squeeze out any excess water and allow the velvet to dry a little before ironing on the reverse side to restore a smooth pile.

Discharge Paste

Discharge paste can be applied to fabric to bleach out or remove the original color, leaving colors ranging from off-white to pale brown, depending on the dyes being used. By mixing a colorant into the chemical discharge paste, it is possible to remove the original color and insert a new color at the same time. The colorants can be illuminant powders, effect paints, or iron-fix s paints. Discharge paste should always be applied to the right si of silk-viscose velvet to ensure the color is effectively removed from the pile and the discharge process is activated by steamin

How to Apply Discharge Paste to Silk-viscose Velvet

Patterns worked using discharge paste.

It is not necessary, particularly if you are working a blocked or screen-printed design, to use a frame to stretch the velvet. Lay the silk velvet pile side up on some protective plastic sheeting and hold in place with masking tape. If using a frame, pin the velvet onto the frame, remembering to have the pile side uppermost. The discharge paste, which is usually white unless mixed with colorants, can be applied from an applicator bottle, brushed on with a firm brush, applied through a screen, or printed from blocks and stamps. A screen-printing frame with a blank screen-printing mesh is very useful for creating an abstract pattern. Scrunch up colored or black velvet and place the blank screen over this fabric, then squeegee the discharge paste through this to create a broke striped effect (see the project on page 94). Apply the paste and leave it to dry, or dry with a hairdryer.

When the fabric is dry, use either a steam iron on the reverse of the velvet to activate the process or roll up the fabric as described on page 16. Steam the parcel for between 2 minutes to approximately one hour, depending on the type of steaming equipment bein used. The completed discharge or introduction of new color will be revealed after the steaming process. The fabric should then be thoroughly washed in cool water to remove all traces of the spent discharge paste and any residue traces of colorants. Allow the fabric to dry off a little before ironing on the wrong side to restore the lie of the pile.

Silk-painting and Shibori Techniques Fixed in a Microwave

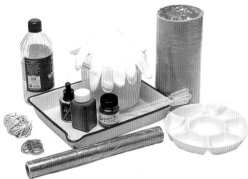

Materials and equipment used for fixing in a microwave.

Using a microwave to fix silk dyes in a range of abstract and semicontrolled patterns is relatively new way of working that does not involve the use of any outliner mediums. This process will only work with steam-fix or acid dyes and is not suitable for working with heat-set paints. The use of vinegar is essential for acid dyes and can be included even if the steam-fix dyes that you are using do not require acidic conditions to set the color. It is a great fun, hands-on approach that can also be enjoyed by children under supervision. It is especially suitable for Shibori work, a traditional Japanese form of dyeing that involves pleating, folding, twisting, wrapping, or stitching fabric using bindings of fine threads or string to create a range of restrictions in the fabric that influence or control the flow of the dye.

In conventional steam-setting methods, the dry, finished work is rolled up and protected by absorbent paper or cotton fabric to prevent crosspatterning during the fixing process. Fixing colors in the microwave is completely different as the work must be wet during the process to encourage the colors to mix and blend until set.

CREATING A RANGE OF ABSTRACT AND SEMICONTROLLED PATTERNS USING A MICROWAVE

In addition to steam-fix dyes, you will need the following equipment to enable you to work a selection of patterns ranging from the complete abstract to Japanese Shibori-style patterns.

Materials

Silk fabric
steam-fix or acid dyes—a maximum of five colors per project is a good guide
white vinegar
a shallow dish
rubber gloves
plastic bands
cotton string
plastic pipettes

water pot and mixing palette
kitchen paper
thick cardboard tube about 4 in. (11 cm) in diameter and 8 in. (20 cm) long, wrapped with clingfilm
plastic sheeting to protect the work area
microwave pot with a ventilated lid or some microwave clingfilm
microwave oven

WORKING PATTERNS IN THE MICROWAVE

Although the patterns vary, the principles for creating them remain the same. No silk-painting frame is needed and the silk should be arranged in its correct formation and soaked in vinegar before the dyes are applied. Whether the vinegar is applied before or after the fabric is arranged depends on the pattern to be worked. For example, it is very difficult to fold a wet piece of silk neatly because the silk sticks to itself. It is therefore much easier to fold the silk into neat squares before applying the vinegar. See the table below to help you to prepare the fabric and apply the vinegar in the correct sequence for a selection of patterns.

Pattern to be Worked	Preparation Before the Application of the Dyes	
Softly marbled pattern	wet silk with vinegar	arrange the silk in contours
Chevron pattern	twist the silk dry	soak with vinegar
Folded patterns	fold the silk dry	soak the folded silk in vinegar
Pleated patterns	pleat the silk dry	soak the pleated silk in vinegar
Ruched patterns	wet the silk with vinegar	ruche up the wet silk
Stitched patterns	insert threads into dry silk	soak the drawn-up silk in vinegar
Knotted patterns	knot the silk dry	soak the knotted silk in vinegar
Arashi patterns	roll and bind dry silk on a tube	roll the silk into a vinegar bath

Once the fabric has been arranged and soaked with vinegar, following the sequence in the above table, the dyes should be applied using plastic pipettes. Remember to spend time beforehand planning, preparing, mixing, and diluting the colors selected for each project. Once applied to the silk, the colors are worked into the fabric using a squeezing, rolling, or pressing action with your hands. The more the silk is handled, the more blended the colors become. The work should always be wrapped loosely in clingfilm or placed in a microwave pot for the cooking and fixing process.

Marbled-effect microwave pattern.

CHEVRON OR FEATHERED PATTERNS

Twist the silk into a skein and place the skein into the vinegar. Apply the colors in bands across the skein, remembering to really press the colors through all of the layers right into the center of the skein. Carefully peek into the center of the skein to check that the color has penetrated to the center.

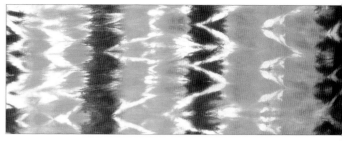

Zigzag-chevron microwave pattern.

FOLDED PATTERNS

Fold the dry silk into neat squares or oblongs and place it in the vinegar. Apply the colors to the top surface, then turn the silk over and reapply the dyes to the underside. Press the dyes down through all of the layers of the silk. Check that they have penetrated all of the layers before fixing.

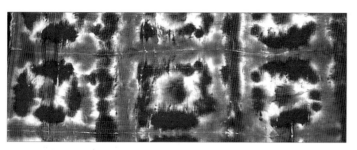

Repeated pattern from folding.

PLEATED DESIGNS

Pleat the silk using your hands, running stitches, or an iron, and place it in the vinegar. Make sure that you only apply the dyes along the edges of the pleat if you want to retain an undyed area across the middle of each pleat. Place the colored pleat carefully into a shallow dish to avoid crosscoloring during the cooking process. Keep your work area especially clean if you want to retain some areas of the silk as white.

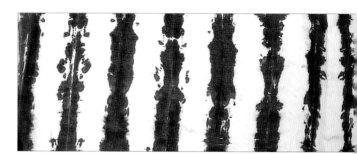

Interesting stripes from pleating.

PLEATED-AND-BOUND PATTERNS

Pleat the silk as before, but then wrap string around the pleat in a neat or crisscross way. Dip the bound pleat into vinegar before applying the colors and pressing them through all of the layers.

More detailed patterns formed by using string.

RUCHED PATTERNS

Immerse the silk in the vinegar, squeeze out the excess, and roughly open out the silk onto the plastic. Start at one end and ruche up the silk in small gathers with your fingers. Apply the colors with pipettes, but work the color in by pressing downward so that you do not disturb the gathers. Try to keep the silk in these gathers as you place it in the pot for steaming.

Colors softly merging along the lines of ruching.

TINY PLEATS AND STITCHED PATTERNS

While the silk is dry, insert a series of small running stitches across the work in patterns of your choosing. You can use a smocking machine to create fine pleats by inserting many threads at once if you have this specialist tool. Draw up the threads before you apply the colors. Wash the dyed fabric and allow it to dry completely before removing the threads if you want to retain the pleated effect.

KNOTTED PATTERNS

Knot the silk across the whole piece and apply the colors to the tip of the knot, on the knot, around the knot, and inside the knot to achieve colored rings. Make sure that you give the colored knots a good squeeze to make the colors penetrate the whole depth of the knot. Do not make the knots too tight as this may restrict the movement of color.

To set the steam-fix dyes, place the work in a ventilated pot, loosely wrap it in clingfilm, and cook it in a microwave set at medium power. Cooking times are based on the size and weight of the piece of silk. Small pieces of lightweight silk of approximately 10 in. (25 cm) in size should only need two minutes. Pieces up to approximately 40 in. (100 cm) in size will need four minutes. A silk blouse approximately 30 in. (75 cm) will need six to eight minutes. Increase the cooking time by a couple of minutes per 40 in. or meter, but always ensure that the silk fabric remains wet while it is in the microwave. The dyes are set when they no longer bleed into new patterns. Keeping the silk damp throughout the cooking process prevents the silk from overheating and becoming scorched. For timings above four minutes, the additional cooking time can be given in two- to three-minute bursts, which allows you to check and adjust the wetness by spraying the work with more vinegar if necessary.

Once the dyes are set, the silk should be washed in warm water with a little liquid detergent to remove any traces of vinegar. Iron while the silk is still damp to remove any creases. This way of working is particularly effective on pongee, habotai, georgette, crepe de chine, and chiffon silks, and is featured in the project on page 66.

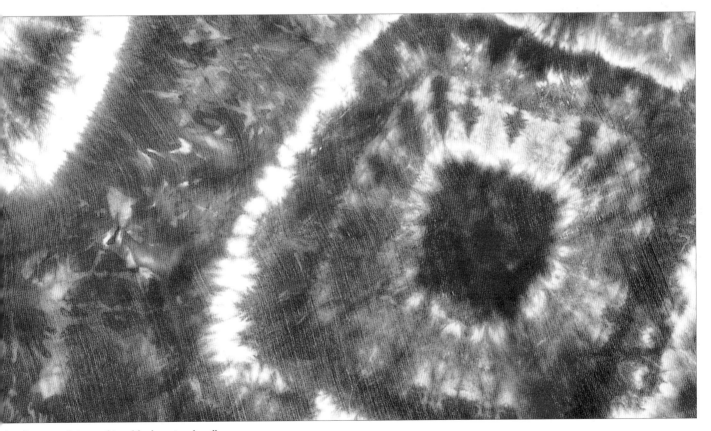

Colored patterned rings achieved by knotting the silk.

Working Arashi Patterns in the Microwave

Arashi Shibori patterns are formed by wrapping or twisting fabric around a tube or pole. Arashi styles can be effectively worked in the microwave using a thick, cardboard tube covered in clingfilm. Since the arrangement of the silk influences the pattern, any fold in the fabric will give a change of direction or repeat the pattern lines created by the bindings. If the fold is on the diagonal, the finished pattern line will change direction at the fold point, creating a "V" shape, whereas folding the silk in half will repeat the pattern equally on each of the folded sides.

This can be useful when working a long scarf as folding the scarf in half end to end before rolling the silk onto the tube will ensure that both the pattern and the colors will be the same at both ends. Rolling the silk onto the tube from the folded edge allows the ends of the scarf to be on the outermost surface on the tube, resulting in a slightly greater depth of color if the dyes are not worked through all of the layers. Alternatively, starting at one end and rolling the silk onto the tube can give a variation of both pattern and color strength throughout the length of the scarf. Don't roll the silk on too tightly as this makes it difficult to ruche up and bind the silk to get the whole width of scarf onto the roll. Twisting the silk on the tube also adds a variation to the lines formed, and it is worth trying different methods of wrapping and binding the silk to create a range of pattern effects.

The tightness and thickness of the string used to bind the silk can also influence the finished pattern. If the string is too fine or too loose, the dye will track under the string, leaving no obvious pattern lines. The thickness and twist of the string can also affect the pattern lines, so experiment with different types to see which produces the most pleasing effect. Variations on the pattern lines formed by the string can be made by reusing string that still contains unfixed dye. Alternatively, try dipping a length of string into dye and allowing it to dry before using it to bind the work. Any unfixed dye left in the string will create darker or colored pattern lines, whereas clean, new string will create paler pattern lines.

Once the silk is wrapped around the tube, it is initially held place with an elastic band at one end, then the tube is bound with string to form the pattern lines. Slip the string under the elastic band and bind it around the tube, placing each strand an equal distance apart before ruching up a section of about $1^1/4$ in (3 cm) at a time. For more dramatic, stormy pattern lines, first ruche up a section of silk, then bind it in place, winding string around with a much more random spacing, allowing the string to cross over itself. Continue binding around the tube, ruching up the bound section, until the whole width of scarf has been worked onto the roll, holding the final end of string in place with another elastic band.

The bound silk should then be rolled in the vinegar tray and any excess squeezed out before placing it on some kitchen paper to prevent the silk roll from sitting in a puddle of vinegar and dye. The colors are applied with pipettes and worked through all of the layers using gloved hands. Further color can be applied to strengthen the depth or change the color blends. Don't worry if the colors look as though they have all merged together. This pressing action must be thorough to ensure that the dye penetrates all of the layers.

Once blended, the colors are set by loosely wrapping the work in clingfilm and cooking it in a microwave for the appropriate time. When setting work on tubes, split the cooking time in half so that the work can be repositioned by rotating the tube part way through the setting process. Additional patterning can be applied with decorative liners, following the contours of these Arashi patterns. (See the project on page 68 for this technique.)

Wrap the folded silk around the tube at an angle for a chevron pattern.

Bind the string neatly for even patterning.

Ruche up a bound section to draw more silk on to the tube.

The finished Arashi pattern, with a chevron directional flow.

PRIMARY COLORS

Red, yellow, and blue are traditionally regarded as the primary colors, that is, colors that cannot be mixed from others, but when themselves mixed together produce a full spectrum. A far wider range of colors can be achieved if two of each of the primary colors are selected for color-mixing. A good selection to start with would be a lemon yellow and a golden yellow; a magenta red and a vermilion (orange red); a cyan (turquoise) and an ultramarine blue.

SECONDARY COLORS

Mixing together two of the primary colors in equal quantities will create secondary colors of orange, green, and violet.

Yellow + red = orange.   Yellow + blue = green.   Red + blue = violet

Since each of the six basic colors lean toward one end of the color wheel or spectrum, a good selection of secondary colors can be achieved. For example, a golden yellow leans toward an orange in the color wheel, whereas a lemon yellow leans toward a yellow green. This means that a richer orange will be achieved using a golden yellow rather than a lemon yellow, but a lemon yellow mixed with a cyan would be a better choice for bright greens.

INTERMEDIATE, OR TERTIARY, COLORS

Mixing together a secondary color with its nearest primary color on the color wheel will give an intermediate, or tertiary, color. A golden yellow mixed with orange will give yellow orange, for example.

COMPLEMENTARY COLORS

Complementary, or opposite, colors are those that sit opposite each another on the color wheel and give the greatest degree of contrast to each other.

The complementary of yellow = violet.   The complementary of red = green.

The complementary of blue = orange.

WARM AND COOL COLORS

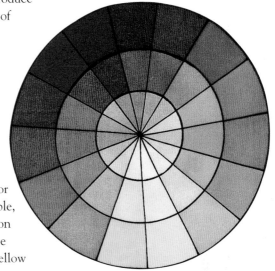

The color wheel, showing a spectrum of colors.

Colors can be grouped in one of the above categories. Reds, oranges, and yellows are considered to be warm colors that appear to come forward in a design, while greens, blues, and violets are cool colors that appear to retreat or recede. This optical effect can be used to add further impact to a piece of work.

The selection of a particular color, or group of colors, obviously affects the appearance of a piece of work. Work a small design in a range of colors, then repeat the design, but change the colors used and compare the results. If you feel uncertain about which colors go together, start looking around you. It may be a border of flowers, someone's outfit, some packaging, or an arrangement in a store window. Take a look at how colors are used and try to analyse why some make such an effective combination.

Cool colors.

Warm colors.

HUE, VALUE, AND INTENSITY

Hue is the name given to a color, for example, red or yellow. Value refers to the lightness or darkness of a hue, or color, in relation to black and white. Since there is no white dye in silk painting, add water to the color to achieve a tint, add gray for a tone, and black to achieve a shade.

Intensity refers to the vibrancy or subtlety of a color. A pure color or hue can be reduced or subdued by mixing a little complementary color (the opposite color on the color wheel) to reduce its intensity. Adding further quantities of the complementary color will create earth colors.

Outline Control With Tint and Tone Exercise

Showing tints and tones.

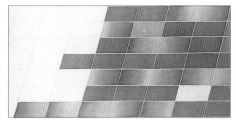

Color filling to form tints and tones.

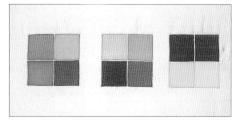

Warm and cool colors, mixed.

Marking out with plastic canvas and a vanishing pen.

A bridge formed with wooden blocks to support the rule just above the silk.

This simple exercise can be worked purely as a sampler or enlarged to create a lovely scarf that gently graduates from one color to a lighter tint or darker tone, creating an attractive, abstract, block pattern. It enables you to practice outlining and working with color. Work this with either heat- or steam-fix dyes on a 10 in. (25 cm) square of silk. Refer to the relevant sections for more informatin on any point.

1. Pin the silk onto the frame to give a taut, even surface.

2. Use a plastic canvas grid to help mark out the corner points and line spacing. Using clear outliner, carefully draw an outline around the edge of the silk to form a border. Remember to keep the end of the nozzle in contact with the silk and to adjust the squeeze to control the outline.

3. Form a bridge with supports on either side of the frame and a long meter rule or yard stick. Run the edge of the nozzle along the edge of the rule to draw a series of straight lines equally distanced apart across the piece of silk. Remember to start and finish the outlines on the outside edge of the border line so that the start and stop blobs, if you have them, will not show when the work is completed.

4. Dry these horizontal lines and turn the frame 90°.

5. Repeat the outlining process, spacing the lines farther apart to form an oblong block pattern. The intersecting lines can be drawn to form a brick-wall pattern, set diagonally to form parallelograms or offset for a more irregular design.

6. Select one primary color and place a measured quantity into three palette wells using a pipette dropper. Leave one well at full strength, dilute the second with an equal quantity of water, and dilute the third with three-quarters water to one-quarter of color.

7. Mix a gray using two complementary colors, for example, yellow and violet, and place this into a fourth palette well.

8. Select a paintbrush and apply the color in a random pattern sequence to one block a time, working from the palest tint to the full-strength color. Always remember to dry your brush after each rinse to prevent further dilution of the color as you work and blend the colors.

9. Repeat this process, but now work from the full-strength color to a darker tone by gradually adding a little gray as you work.

10. Continue to fill all of the shapes, varying the shading from full-strength color to pale tints on some blocks and from full-strength color to darker tones on others.

11. Finally, use the complementary color in some of the blocks to act as a highlight and add strength to the overall effect.

12. When the grid is completed, allow the dyes to dry and then fix the paints or dyes in the appropriate way. Please refer to pages 15–16 for information on the fixing process.

13. Once the work is fixed, wash the silk to remove the clear outliner, then iron it while it is still damp to restore the full sheen and movement of the silk.

Silk-painting Sampler

aving assembled the necessary equipment and materials, and
acticed mixing some colors, you are ready to start your first
k-painting project. This 10 in. (25 cm) square sampler project
es a range of different techniques and allows you to discover
e delights of silk painting while providing a good reference
int for all of your future pieces. It can be worked with either
at- or steam-fix colors.

This patchwork sampler is also a good way of working for a
oup activity with adults or children who each want to
ntribute a little something to the overall piece.

Pin the silk to the frame to give a taut, even surface (see
page 22).

Holding the outliner tube or applicator bottle in the correct
way, draw a freehand, double line around the edge of the silk
to form a border and then subdivide the working area into a
selection of smaller shapes. They do not have to be equal in
size or be a drawing of a particular shape, they just need to
provide a selection of large and smaller enclosed shapes.
Remember to consider using a selection of outline colors (see
page 24 for drawing outlines).

Dry the outlines with a hairdryer.

Select a range of colors and place them in your palette with a
pipette dropper.

Apply the colors with a brush of an appropriate size for the
area to be filled, remembering to allow the color to spread
across the silk (see page 28).

Try blending some colors together within a shape.

Try diluting some colors with water from a pure, full-strength
color to a lighter tint.

Apply spots of color or small amounts of either alcohol or
water to create further patterning on damp, colored areas.
Use a hairdryer to dry this patterning at the right time.

Mix a little thickener with some color and apply this to your
sampler. When dry, add color around the shape, allowing it
to run up to the edge of the thickened pattern line (see
page 27).

0. Apply color to a shape and, while the area is still damp,
sprinkle some salt-effect crystals onto the wet surface. Work
one shape at a time to ensure that the silk does not dry too
much before the salt is added (see page 34).

11. Select a slightly larger brush and apply the color to the
border area. Remember to apply paint to both leading edges
of the color, working alternately from one side to the other so
that one edge does not dry and form an unwanted watermark.

12. Dry the piece of completed work and fix in the appropriate
way for the type of silk paint or dye used for this project.
Please refer to pages 15–16 for details on the fixing process.

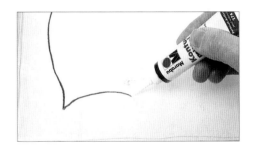

Drawing a freehand border using a tube of outliner.

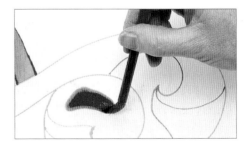

Applying the color to the center of the shape and allowing it to spread to the outline.

Applying spots of water to damp silk to form patterns.

Brushing down colored thickener to create further patterning.

Planning a Design

Creating an impressive piece of finished work does not just involve a high level of technical expertise in the execution of the outlining and application of dyes, it also involves good design. What makes a good design is partly a personal view, but considering certain factors can help. Borders and edges are particularly important on scarves, for example, as these are the areas that will be most visible when the scarf is being worn. A border gives an opportunity to introduce another color, possibly a complementary hue, a color that you have already used in the piece, or a tone or shade of one of the colors already used. The border itself does not have to look like a frame mount as it can be softened by allowing the design to spill out over or behind it. Consider using the actual pattern motifs to create a border by overlapping and placing the patterns at the edge of the work.

Use a variety of design source materials to work up designs.

Achieving even coloring on large, complicated, background areas is often considered to be one of the most difficult facets of silk painting. Reduce the background or largest area by linking pattern shapes together to minimize the number of isolated shapes. Shapes can be joined by overlapping, making leaves or stalks touch, grouping shapes into clusters, or allowing shapes to touch the edge of the piece.

The placement of shapes is also important. Do not feel that a piece always has to have a mirror image or that you have to place an identical pattern in each corner to achieve balance. This is just one option; also consider rotating the design, working the same design in different sizes, repeating just part of the pattern, or leaving an area plain. The negative shapes and spaces have just as much importance to the design as the areas that have pattern detail or images. Achieving balance could involve using shapes or colors to create a harmony within the piece, a focal point, or images that lead your eye around the whole design.

If you feel unsure about your drawing skills, try using designs from pattern books, or look at nature for inspiration, experimenting with color combinations and shapes that appeal to you. You do not need to copy these images exactly; change them slightly or combine them with your own ideas and patterns. Try to develop your observational and drawing skills, and, with practice, your confidence and skills will improve.

The selection of projects featured in this book can be worked from the patterns supplied at the back of the book and by following the accompanying step-by-step instructions. Photocop these designs to a size that will fit your piece of silk and use som of these suggestions to personalize them.

Shells, feathers, and leaves provide interesting shapes.

Applying Further Surface Decoration

Having completed a silk painting, you may wish to add more embellishment or decoration using some of the paints, decorative liners, and foils, not to mention charms, beads, and sequins available to the textile artist. All of these are best applied to the projects featured in this book once the painting has been fixed and washed to allow a good bonding with the silk. Why not try adding some of these to enhance some of your projects?

GLITTER LINERS

Glitter liners are heat set and can be applied directly from the nozzle on the tube in the same way as a resist line. They appear slightly milky when initially applied, but give a glitter effect when dry. They work very effectively as a delicate highlight when applied lightly along the pattern lines of Arashi patterning to give a hint of sparkle or used to add further interest to images formed on velvet with heat-stamping.

PUFF LINERS AND PAINT MEDIUMS

Puff liners and paint mediums are applied in the same way as glitter liners or can be brushed or sponged on. When dry, they can be puffed up with dry heat from an iron, hairdryer, or heat tool as appropriate. Puff liners or paint mediums can also be used to hold small beads or sequins to the surface of the silk.

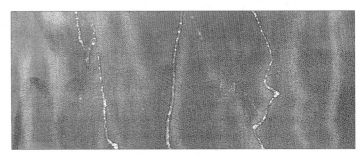

Glitter liner.

Puff liner.

DECORATIVE FOILS

Available in a wide range of colors, decorative foils give a wonderful metallic finish that works particularly well as a linear highlighter on velvet, but is also effective on many other surfaces. Cellophane foils are bonded to the silk with glue or bondaweb and give a flexible, washable finish. Special glue, either a plexiglue or appliglue, is first drawn onto the silk in a line from an applicator bottle. Initially, the glue appears milky, but it becomes transparent as it dries. When the glue is transparent, lay a piece of foil, color side uppermost, on top of the glue line and press lightly with a finger to transfer the foil down to the glue. These foils can also be applied with bondaweb for larger patches of foiling. Iron the bondaweb onto the fabric, then use the warm iron flat, or the edge of the iron, to transfer the foils to the bondaweb area with a pressing action.

Foils on devorée velvet.

A selection of foils and plexiglue

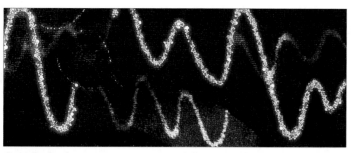

Granular beads.

GRANULAR BEADS

Tiny, granular beads can be sprinkled onto wet plexi- or appliglue and allowed to dry to give a beautiful, textured finish. Any loose beads can be shaken off the fabric and returned to the pot for later use. This is more suitable for a decorative effect for items that will only require occasional hand-washing.

A charm bee.

BEADS, CHARMS, SHISHA MIRRORS, AND SEQUINS

There is now a wonderful selection of small attachments like beads, charms, shisha mirrors, and sequins, which can add detail to the designs or along the edges or corners of work. They can be stuck with puff mediums or easily sewn onto the silk with either a fine silk or polyester thread.

Charms, sequins, and shisha mirrors.

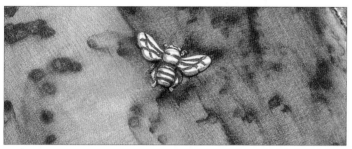

Hot-stamping blocks.

HOT-STAMPING ON PILED FABRICS

It is possible to produce some stunning effects in piled fabrics using rubber stamps or linoblocks with which to press down the pile and create a relief pattern in the fabric. Take a commercial available stamping block like the hot-potato range, or make you own stamp by cutting a design into a piece of printing lino with lino-cutting tools. Lay the block down, pattern side uppermost, and position the silk velvet pile side down on the block. Spray little water on the back of the velvet and then place a flat iron on the back of the velvet. (Steam irons may create hole marks on the fabric from the underside of the iron sole plate, so are no suitable.) Hold in place for 15 seconds, then remove the iron and check the pattern impression. The use of water helps to protect the fabric while it is being heated and creates some steam, which helps to form the impression. Patterns worked with this method provide a decorative effect that will not withstand washing as the pile will revert to its original position.

A hot-stamped sampler.

Silk-painting Projects

hese projects cover a range of skill levels, using a selection of silk-painting techniques, ints, and dyes. The most simple projects are at the beginning and progress to more hallenging works, allowing you to develop your silk-painting skills. It is usually possible to bstitute a different dye to the one featured in the project if you wish, but remember to take to account any changes needed, particularly in the fixing process.

The step-by-step instructions provide the sequence of working, but if you need further formation or clarification, refer to the earlier chapters, which describe the materials and chniques in detail.

Freesia Scarf

This is a lovely project that can be painted successfully and with confidence by novices. The outlining is completely worked with a clear resist and the background is left unpainted. This ensures that any thick outlines or blobs accidentally formed as the lines are drawn do not show in the completed piece. Painting the freesias provides good practice in mixing and applying tints and gives the completed piece a delicate and realistic feeling that will inspire you to continue.

Equipment and Materials

Ready-edged pongee or habotai scarf or piece of silk

Heat-fix dyes

Clear heat-fix outliner

Frame and silk pins

Paintbrushes

Mixing palette and water pot

Kitchen paper

Iron for setting the paints

Template (page 102)

Tip: remember to hold the tube at about 45° and keep the nozzle tip in contact with the silk while applying very light pressure to control the flow of the outliner.

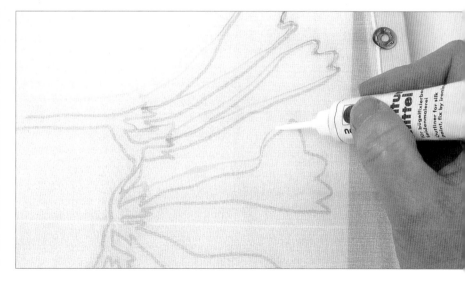

1. Assemble the frame to fit the piece of silk and fasten the fabric to the frame with silk pins.

2. Place a selection of the photocopied patterns under the silk, moving them around until you create a pleasing arrangement. Try overlapping, grouping, or fanning out the shapes to fit the piece of silk. Look through the silk to follow the patterns and trace out all of the freesias onto the silk using the clear outliner. Only use light pressure to squeeze the tube, and keep a piece of kitchen paper handy to wipe the nozzle tip.

Use a hairdryer to dry the outliner.
move all of the photocopied patterns
m under the work frame.

4. Using pipettes, select a range of colors
and prepare a few tints by diluting some
of the colors with water.

5. Use a brush to apply the color,
allowing the paint to run to the outline.
While the color is still damp, add a
little water to push the color to the
outline to give halo shading, or blend
a lighter tint with the deeper color to
give blended shading.

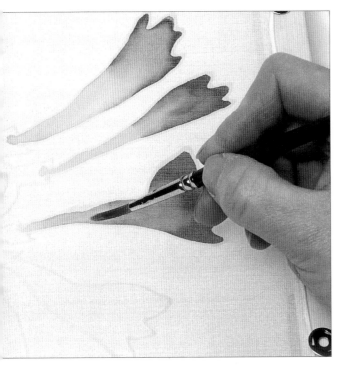

. Continue painting in all of the flowers, one stem at a time,
then add a little green for the stalks.

7. Use a fine brush and remember to allow for the spread of
the paint to ensure that the green does not run into the
flower heads too much. Remember not to paint in any of
the background.

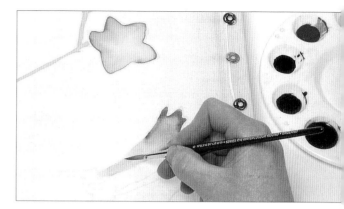

8. Create natural shading with tints.

9. Create halo shading using water.

10. When the painting is complete, allow the work to dry. Before unpinning the work, check that the table underneath the frame is clean and that there are no drops paint. Fix the work with an iron on a wool setting, ironing on the reverse side of the silk for about three minutes acros the whole piece, or fix in the appropriate way if other pain were used. Wash the fixed piece in warm water with a little liquid detergent to remove the clear outliner. Reiron the silk while it is still damp to bring out the full sheen of the silk and give a beautiful finish to your completed scarf.

Silk-painted Cards

Equipment and Materials

- Heat-fix paints
- Frame and silk pins
- Piece of silk
- Water pot and mixing palette
- Selection of brushes
- Pattern motifs
- Iron to set the colors
- For mounting:
- Window-aperture cards or quality cartridge paper
- Craft knife
- Sharp scissors
- Stick adhesive
- Double-sided tape
- Wadding for padded cards
- Silk outliner or metallic pen
- Template (page 103)

Cards are a lovely way of developing skills as they can incorporate many techniques on a smaller scale, which makes everything seem less daunting. Heat-fix paints are the ideal choice for cards because they are so easy to fix. The patterns featured at the back of the book can be used to make a selection of greetings and occasion cards, and there are suggestions for mounting to provide a variety of ways of presenting the finished work.

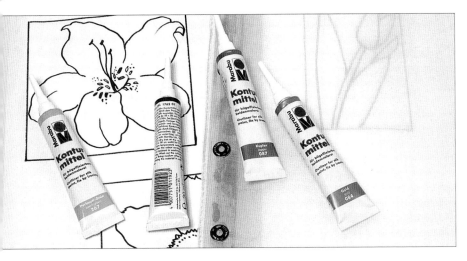

1. Assemble the frame, pin out the silk, and place the selected pattern under the work as described in the freesia project. When working cards, it can be helpful to divide the area of silk into boxes using the outliner to allow several cards to be worked from the one piece of silk. This prevents the colors from one card running into another card design that is being worked alongside.

2. Draw out the outlines in a selection of outliner colors. Allow them to dry and remove the pattern sheets before starting to paint in the flower.

3. When the flower has been completed, paint in the background. Start at one corner and work across to the opposite side.

4. Lightly sprinkle salt crystals onto the wet silk paint if you want to create textured patterns.

5. Leave the work to dry naturally to allow the salt patterns to form.

6. Brush off the salt crystals, iron the work on the reverse side to fix the designs, the wash and reiron while damp to restore a smooth, flat finish ready for mounting.

Surface-mounting

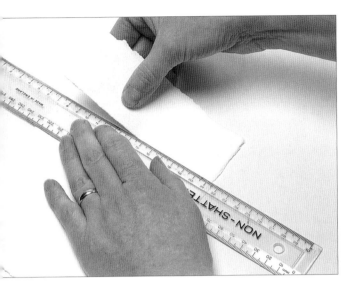

2. A silk design that is to be surface-mounted can be trimmed ready for mounting onto the card front in the following ways to give a variety of finished edge effects:

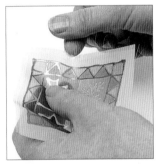

- If the design has an outline around the edge, the silk can be cut along this line, giving a neat, no-fray edge.
- The silk can be trimmed just inside an outlined edge and then carefully frayed back for about ¹/₄ in. (50 mm) to give a fringe effect along each of the edges.
- The silk can be trimmed just outside the outlined edge and then carefully frayed back to the outliner edge, which will prevent any further fraying.

. Take a good-quality, ready-folded greetings card or a piece of heavyweight cartridge or watercolor paper and cut or tear it carefully into a rectangle of your chosen size. Fold the rectangle in half, pressing along the folded edge to form a folded card. Tearing the edges gives a more interesting effect, but they can be cut with a craft knife if a smooth edge is preferred.

Tip: make sure that your card will fit into a standard envelope.

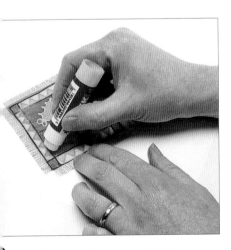

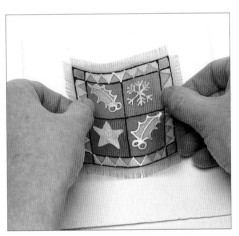

3. Apply a small amount of stick adhesive on the wrong side of the piece of silk, cut to size in one of the above ways. Take special care not to get any glue on the fringe or front of the design.

4. Position the silk over the card front, then carefully lower it into position and secure it by pressing firmly across the surface.

5. Allow to dry before adding any further detailing or wording with the heat-fix outliners or a metallic pen.

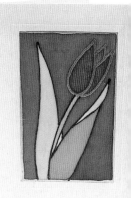

Variations: surface-mounting techniques can be applied to other shapes beside the basic square and rectangle. Any shapes with a heat-fix-outliner edge can be cut out along the outliner edge, which seals the edge and prevents further fraying.

The no-fray edging technique can also be scaled up and used to finish a scarf or sarong without the need for any sewing. It can be effective if you add a little wadding to pad out your finished design. Follow the steps for window-aperture cards, but add a little extra allowance when cutting out the silk to accommodate the wadding. Cut the wadding the same size as the window and place it behind the silk to pad out the design when the card flap is stuck into position.

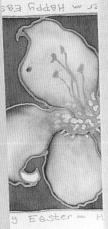

Silk beaded necklace

Equipment and Materials

Piece of silk

Frame and silk pins

Heat-fix dyes

Large paintbrushes

Water pot

Salt-effect crystals

Iron for heat-fixing the paints

Pressed cotton-fiber beads

Pony beads

Sewing equipment

This very simple, but effective, way of making a necklace can be worked in any color combination to make jewelry suitable for any occasion. The simplicity of the project, and the use of salt to create the beautiful, textural patterns, lends itself to working with children or as a clever way of using up small strips of silk or samplers.

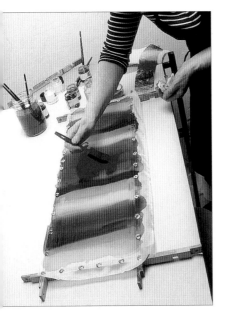

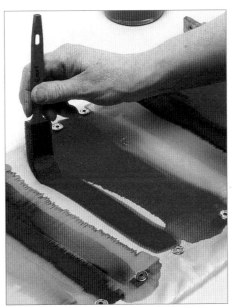

. Assemble the frame to fit a piece of silk approximately 30 in. (75 cm) long and fasten the fabric to the frame with silk pins. Select a range of colors and place them in the mixing palette. Use a large Chinese brush or sponge brush to apply the color in stripes across the silk.

2. Space the stripes so that they just overlap as they spread out. Work quite freely to ensure that the whole piece has plenty of color to prevent quick drying.

3. Check that the silk is still wet before sprinkling salt crystals over the whole piece. To ensure maximum patterning, do not overcrowd the salt crystals.

4. Allow the work to dry naturally, then brush off all of the salt crystals and unpin the silk from the frame.

5. Use an iron to set the colors. Wash the silk in warm water to remove any excess color and salt deposits. Allow to dry and then reiron. Cut the silk into a strip about 28 in. (70 cm) long. The width is determined by the size of the cotton-fiber beads. Measure the circumference of a bead and add a little extra for a seam allowance.

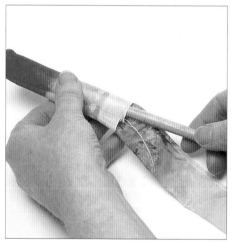

6. Fold the strip into half lengthwise. Pin and tack along the long edge before sewing it up, but leave both ends open.

7. Turn the tube inside out. You may find that a knitting needle helps.

8. Take one of the cotton-fiber beads and insert it down the tube.

Thread one of the small, spacer, pony beads on each end of the tube and push them along until they sit next to the covered bead.

10. Continue inserting cotton-fiber beads and threading spacer beads along the necklace until it is the length you want.

11. Join the open ends of the tube together with a few stitches to complete the necklace.

Silk Potpourri or Lavender Sachets

As you practice the various techniques, you will inevitably produce a few samplers and test pieces, some of which you will not want to keep for reference. Why not use them to make some scented sachets to hang in your closet or place in your clothes drawers? The variation of finishing details is endless and helps to make each sachet an original piece of work.

Equipment and Materials

A completed, fixed, and washed piece of silk

Frame and silk pins

Selection of heat-fix outliners (not clear)

Sewing thread and needle

Selection of beads, charms, sequins, or ribbons for decoration

Potpourri or lavender

Sharp scissors or pinking shears

Meter rule or yard stick

Water-soluble or disappearing pen

Baking or greaseproof paper

Iron for setting the outliners

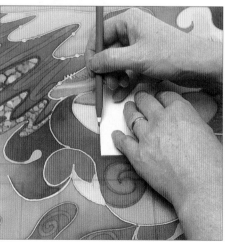

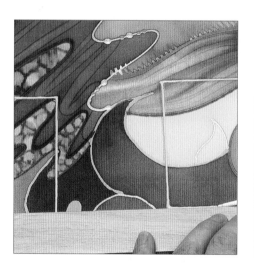

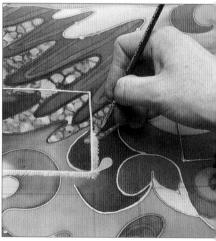

1. Restretch the finished piece of colored silk back onto a frame, securing it with silk pins. Use the disappearing pen to mark out half of the fabric into squares of about 3¹/₂ in. (9 cm).

2. Make a bridge with the meter rule, using some supports to lift the rule just above the silk, and draw out the squares using a heat-fix outliner.

3. Use a brush to spread out the outliner. Don't worry if the lines look untidy as the edges will be trimmed after sewing up.

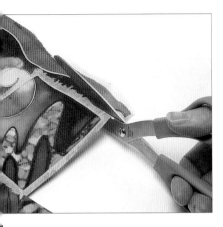

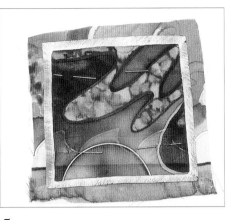

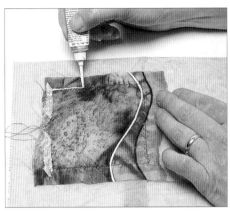

4. Dry the outlines, unpin the dry silk, and then cut out these squares and the remaining fabric, all slightly oversized to make it easier to sew the squares together.

5. Pin an outlined square onto another unmarked square of silk and carefully sew around all of the sides using a small running stitch (or use a sewing machine), leaving a small gap to insert the potpourri. Sew just inside the dry outliner.

6. Lay the sachet on some baking paper and, using the sewing line as a guide, reoutline the other side, then allow it to dry. This will seal the two squares neatly together. When dry, use a sharp pair of scissors or pinking shears to trim the edges.

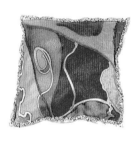

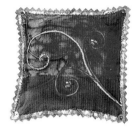

. Fill the sachets with lavender or potpourri, then close the hole with a few more stitches.

. Add further decoration with glitter liners, puff liners, beads, sequins, ribbons, or charms.

Printing With Silk-Paint Thickener

Using silk-paint thickener to form a simple printed design works very well, and is especially suitable for children or anyone who finds it difficult to achieve fine brush control. The printing can be worked from commercially available sponge stamps or you can make your own very effectively from thin polystyrene, which can be cut with scissors or a craft knife. If the background is to be a pale color, it is possible to paint this in as an overall wash first before printing the shapes on top. For darker backgrounds, it is better to print the shapes, then paint in the background around them.

Equipment and Materials

Ready-edged scarf or piece of silk

A frame and silk pins

Heat-fix paints

Heat-fix silk-paint thickener medium

Water pot and mixing palette

Paintbrushes

Ready-made sponge stamps or your own print blocks

Iron for setting the colors

Tip: make sure that you thoroughly mix the paint and thickener together, otherwise the paint may run and spoil the design.

1. Assemble the frame to fit the silk and fasten the silk to the frame with silk pins. Place a small amount of thickener into a well of the mixing palette. Add an equal amount of silk paint to the thickener and thoroughly mix the two together. Repeat this with as many colors as you want to use in your design.

2. Take a stamp and then apply the colored, thickened, silk-paint medium to the stamp.

Several colors can be applied to one stamp for multicolored prints.

4. Carefully press the stamp down onto the stretched silk to achieve a good print. Reapply the thickened color and continue.

5. Here the pattern is applied using a commercial stamp block.

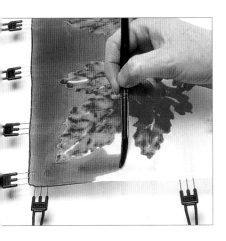

Variations: it is possible to add further detail by using a heat-fix outliner in, and around, the printed shapes. Do not, however, apply the outliner over the top of any of the thickener as the outliner will not be able to bond directly with the fabric and will come away at the washing stage. Alternatively, after fixing and the final wash, which removes the thickener, restretch the silk onto the frame and then apply outliner as surface decoration. You can also substitute steam-fix dyes if you prefer, following the instructions given on page 16 for steam-fixing.

Allow the work to dry before painting in the background color. Use unthickened silk paint to paint the background, but still leave a little spreading distance and allow the paint to run up to the printed shapes. Select the best starting place and paint outward, working around the shapes as you go.

Allow the work to dry, remove it from the frame, and fix by ironing. Wash the fixed work in warm water to remove the water-soluble thickener and any excess color. Allow to dry a little before reironing to give a lovely finish to the silk.

Abstract Patterns Fixed in a Microwave

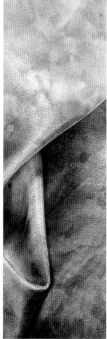

The lovely, soft marbling produced in this technique is easy to work, especially on pongee and habotai silk. As the dyes will mix to produce other colors, remember to choose hues that mix well together and consider introducing a contrast element by using colors of varying tonal strengths.

Equipment and Materials

Ready-edged scarf or piece of lightweight pongee or habotai silk

Steam-fix dyes (a maximum of four or five colors works best)

White vinegar to help set the dyes (essential if you are using acid dyes)

Shallow tray

Mixing palette

Plastic pipettes

Plastic gloves

Piece of plastic to protect the table (clear or white plastic is preferable)

Ventilated microwave pot or bowl and clingfilm

Microwave

Tip: take a little time arranging the fabric, without compacting it too much, as the "hill and valley" contours form the marbled pattern in the silk.

Tip: to avoid tiny dot splash marks, refill the pipette with more color rather than trying to squeeze out the last drop. Tiny splashes of dye can be difficult to blend out and can spoil the completed work.

1. Cover the table with the plastic sheeting. Wearing plastic gloves, pour some vinegar into the shallow tray and immerse the silk. Squeeze out the excess vinegar and place the wet silk on the plastic.

2. Arrange the wet silk into some interesting "hill and valley" contours. The silk will stay in the arrangement you create as it is wet and will cling to itself or the plastic.

3. Use a pipette to lift up the colors and drizzle the dye onto the silk.

Try to distribute the colors evenly across the silk, using light pressure on the bulb of the pipette to release a controlled amount of dye.

5. When all of the colors have been applied, blend them using the tips of your fingers. Try to keep the contours of "hills and valleys." The more you handle the work, the more blended the colors become.

6. Draw the wet silk together, lift it up, and place it in a plastic container, keeping the silk well down in the base of the container. Cover with a ventilated lid and place the container on the microwave turntable.

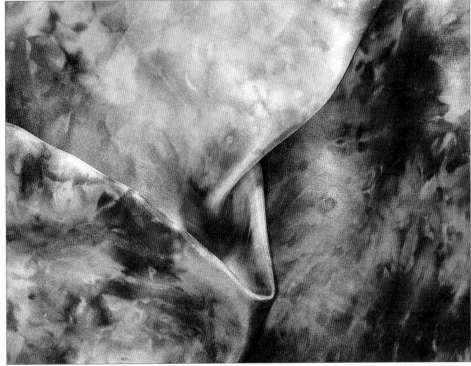

. Turn the microwave to a medium-power setting and cook for four minutes. Remove the container and carefully open the lid to allow the hot, vinegary steam to escape.

Remove the silk and rinse in warm, soapy water to remove any traces of vinegar or excess dye. Iron the silk while it is still damp to remove any creases and give a beautiful finish.

Variations: see pages 42–43 for information on how to create other informal patterns using a microwave to set the steam-fix dyes.

Arashi Shibori Pattern Fixed in the Microwav

The beautiful, translucent qualities of a light pongee or chiffon silk are very well suited to Shibori work; the depth of color and patterns are greatly enhanced by the layering effect as the silk softly drapes back on itself. Finally, further embellishment can be added by attaching small shisha mirrors or fine glitter lines for a little sparkle or evening elegance.

Tip: if you would prefer the stripes to run across the width of the scarf, fold the scarf in half lengthwise, twice, and start wrapping the folded silk around the tube from the ready-rolled edges.

Tip: if you prefer stormy pattern lines, work the binding and wrapping much more freely by pushing up the silk before binding it in place with the string. Taking the string back over itself forms lozenge shapes. The more carefree the binding, the more stormy the resulting pattern becomes.

Equipment and Materials

Long, ready-edged scarf or piec of chiffon or mousseline silk
Steam-fix silk dyes (a maximur of four or five colors works best
White vinegar (essential if usin acid dyes)
Shallow tray (a roasting pan slightly wider than the length of the tube)
Mixing palette
Plastic pipettes
String (new or already colored from previous dyeing)
Elastic bands
Kitchen paper
Plastic gloves
Piece of plastic to protect the table
An approximately 8 in. (20 cm length of thick card tube (carpet-roll tube is ideal)
Clingfilm
Microwave

1. Cover the table with the plastic. Wrap some clingfilm around the cardboard tube to prevent the dyes from staining or wetting the cardboard.

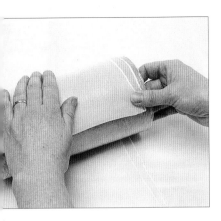

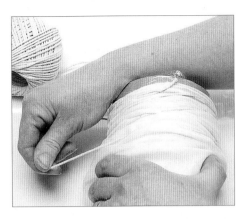

Fold the chiffon in half, end to end for a mirror image. Wrap the folded silk around the tube, starting from the folded edge. This will give pattern lines that run the length of the scarf.

3. Place an elastic band around one end of the tube to hold the rolled silk in place. Slip the end of the string under the elastic band and start winding the string around the tube.

4. If you want neat, evenly spaced lines, wrap the string evenly around the tube for about 3 in. (8 cm), then push this section together to draw the loose end of the silk onto the tube. Continue binding in this way until the silk is completely wrapped and bound around the tube, then secure the end of the string with another elastic band.

. Wearing plastic gloves, pour some vinegar into the shallow tray. Roll the tube with the wrapped silk in the vinegar. Squeeze out any excess and place the wet silk on some kitchen paper. Use pipettes to apply the steam-fix dyes. Drizzle the dye around the silk, following the direction of the string, until the colors have been evenly distributed. Keep the tube on some kitchen paper to soak up any excess puddles of liquid.

6. Press and roll the tube to push the dye down, through the layers of chiffon silk. It is very important to press firmly, even if it looks as though all of the colors have merged together too much. Have confidence as inadequate pressure will result in undyed or poorly patterned areas in the finished work.

7. Loosely wrap the dyed, wet, silk roll in clingfilm and place it on the microwave turntable. The length of the card tube will be dictated by the diameter of the turntable of your microwave.

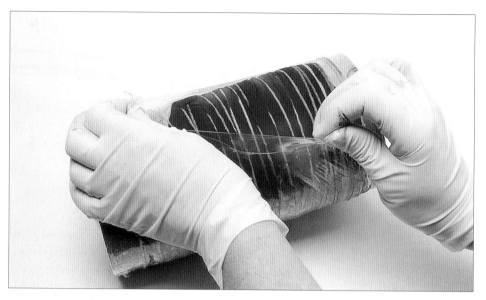

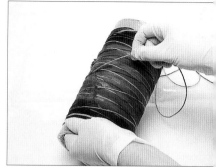

8. Cook the silk for two minutes on a medium-heat setting, open the microwave, rotate to reposition the covered tube, and cook for a further two minutes on a medium setting. This time is suitable for a long, thin or square scarf of about $15\frac{1}{2}$ in.^{2} (1 m^2). When cooked, remove the silk tube from the microwave and carefully unwrap the clingfilm, allowing any steam to escape. Be careful: the silk will be hot.

9. Remove the elastic bands and unwind the string. Check that the dye has penetrated through the layers properly.

[

10. Now wash the scarf in cool, soapy water to remove any excess dye and vinegar. Keep the string for reuse in further projects. Iron the silk while is still damp to restore the shape an softness of the chiffon.

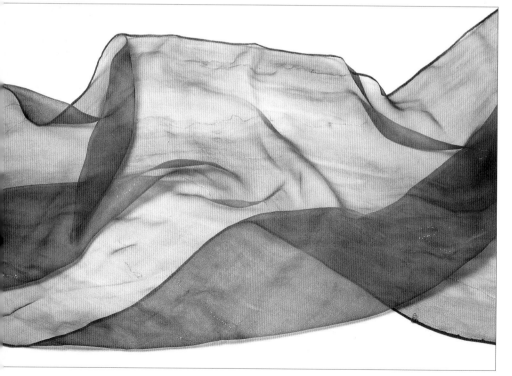

11. If you wish, add a little heat-set glitter liner along the pattern lines sew on some shisha mirrors for a little added sparkle.

Velvet Drape for a Table or Sofa

Equipment and Materials

Long length of white silk-viscose velvet

Selection of procion dyes made up into liquid dyes (see page 37)

Jam jar per color

Soda ash

Large, shallow tray (a marbling tray, cat-litter box, or automobile-oil tray are ideal)

Rubber gloves

Pipettes

Synthrapol (optional)

Some old newspapers

This velvet drape will give a touch of luxury to any table or sofa. The simple method of dyeing in a tray gives lovely results and is an easy introduction to working with procion dyes. Once finished, the drape can be further embellished with any of the decorative media or perhaps finished with some tassels at each corner.

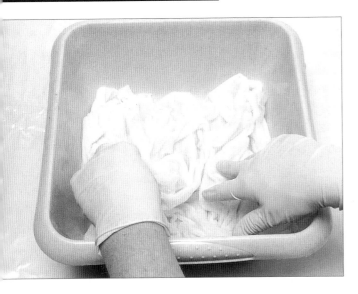

1. Wet the piece of silk velvet in water and squeeze out the excess so that it is just damp. Loosely arrange the velvet in the tray to create some interesting contours.

2. Wearing the rubber gloves, apply the liquid dyes one color at a time, using either a pipette for controlled application or just sloshing on the color for a more random effect.

3. When all of the colors have been applied, use your hands to lightly blend the colors together. Then carefully tip away any excess color to prevent the fabric from sitting in dark pools of dye. Leave the velvet for at least 30 minutes to allow the colors to blend. The longer the velvet is left, and the more it is handled, the more blended the colors become.

4. Mix up the soda ash to make the fixative solution (see page 37) and pour it all over the velvet. Leave the fixative to work for approximately one hour.

5. Tip away the spent fixative solution and dye, then rinse the velvet in cold water. Keep rinsing until the water runs clear. It will take several rinses to achieve this, or use Synthrapol to help rinse out surplus dye. Squeeze out any excess water and then spread the dyed velvet out on newspapers to dry.

6. When the velvet is still just damp, iron it on the wrong side to restore the plush sheen. For a crushed-velvet look, allow the velvet to dry completely before giving it a quick ironing on the reverse side or tumble-drying it on a cool setting.

7. Finish the edges by hand or on a sewing machine, adding embellishment or tassels if you wish.

Chiffon Scarf With Overlaid Color and Watermark Patterns

Equipment and Materials

Two long, silk chiffon or mousseline ready-edged scarves

4 pieces of chiffon silk

Frame and silk pins

Steam-fix dyes

Large brushes

Water pot and mixing palette

Hairdryer

Steam-fixing equipment

This scarf is worked as a double layer of translucent chiffon to give a beautiful, overlaid pattern that is finished with a decorative edge of small beads. Choose colors that will work well together when layered, and consider varying the patterns for different effects.

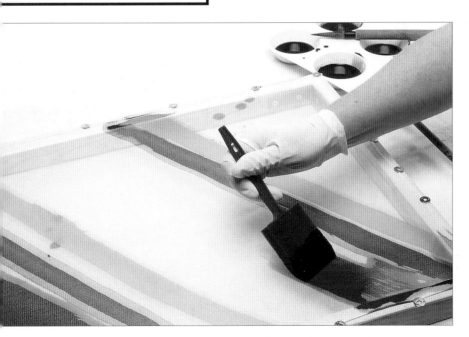

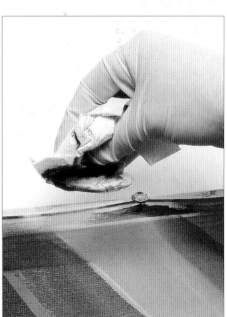

1. Pin out the silk using the silk pins. Place the selected colors into the mixing palette, diluting, if necessary, with water. Apply the dyes to the silk in a diagonal stripe, using a large brush to release a wide band of color. Vary the amount of contact the brush makes with the silk to control the spread of the dye.

2. Dab the wet edges of the scarf with kitchen paper to prevent the dyes from flowing back.

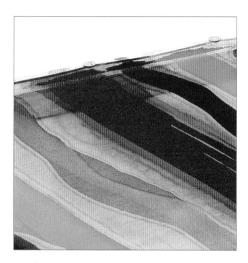

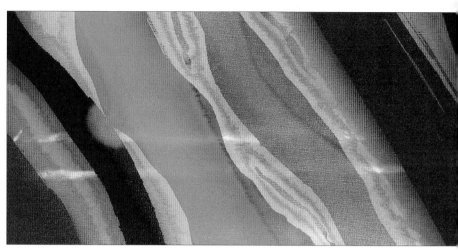

3. Dry the first layer of colors when each of the stripes has merged with its neighbor in a pleasing way. Repeat the application of dye or use water for a lighter effect.

4. This second application of liquid will create some beautiful watermarks. Leave to dry naturally or use a hairdryer for more dramatic patterns. Repeat this coloring process on the second scarf, using different colors. Steam both scarves to set the dyes (see pages 16–19). Wash and iron the scarves.

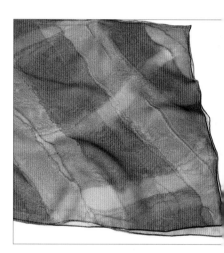

5. Lay one scarf on top of the other to see the crossover patterns formed. Try all of the pattern-overlay possibilities by moving the scarf around before deciding which one works most effectively.

6. Sew the two scarves together along the rolled edge with a fine thread.

7. Finish the scarf with a line of bead along each bottom edge to add a little sparkle and weight to the completed item.

Variations: try sandwiching some frayed silk-organza shapes between the layers or add outliner or glitter liner to decorate the scarf further.

Silk Sarong

Equipment and Materials

Two long, bamboo garden canes slightly longer than the length of the sarong

Two bamboo garden canes slightly longer than the width of the sarong

Reel of masking tape

Clothes pegs

Regular frame and silk pins or a large embroidery hoop

Heat-fix silk paints (three or four colors work well)

Three or four pump-action spray bottles, one per color

Heat-fix outliners

Heat-fix silk-paint thickener

Piece of natural sponge

Paintbrushes

Mixing palette and water pot

Hairdryer

Pattern motifs

Plastic sheeting or newspaper to protect the floor

Iron to set the colors or dry-cure in an oven

Template (page 104)

This project shows how easy it can be to work a large length of silk without the need for a specialist frame. The silk is pegged onto garden bamboo canes taped together and supported on chairs, table ends, or sawhorses, worked either outside on a sunny day or over a floor area protected by plastic sheeting. Working a much larger piece is good practice, great fun, and helps to give spontaneity to the work. The paints are sprayed on in this project, with the patterns formed using thickener and outliner. The completed project makes a lovely sarong or silk wrap.

1. Assemble the bamboo canes into a frame large enough to take the piece of silk, crossing over the ends of the canes and taping them securely together with masking tape. Support each end of the assembled frame on suitable supports (as suggested above) and cover the floor with plastic if you are working inside.

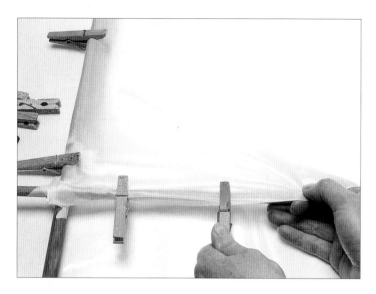

2. Start at one corner and fasten the silk onto the canes using clothes pegs. You should be able to achieve a reasonable tension, and it does not have to be as tight as you may normally work.

3. Place some silk-paint thickener into a large palette well and dip in the sponge. Lightly sponge the thickener onto the silk in arc patterns to form waves. Do not sponge too heavily or you will have solid areas of thickener. Dry the thickener with a hairdryer or allow it to dry naturally while you mix up the paints.

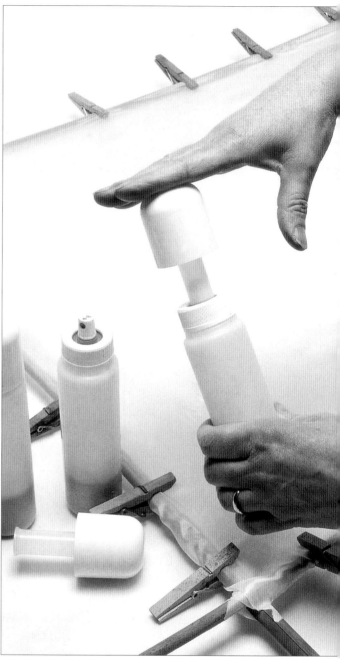

4. Prepare two of the pump-action bottles using 10 pipettes of color for the two dominant colors in the project. Prepare the remaining pump-action bottles using five pipettes of color for the accent colors. Dilute each of the bottles with a good quantity of water and test the depth of color on a scrap of silk. Adjust if necessary, but keep the colors pale to mid-strength so that the colors of the motifs applied later will still show.

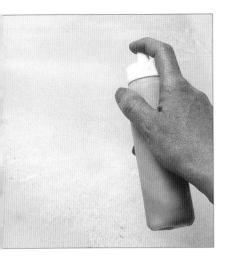

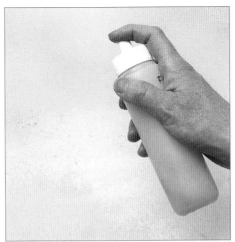

Spray the colors onto the silk, initially spraying around the thickener shapes to allow the paints to flow up and into the printed waves.

6. Change over the colors as you spray, wet on wet to give a blended effect, and then lightly spray over the printed waves to pick out the open-textured detail. Work freely, and quite quickly, until the whole area has been colored.

7. If the paints are still damp, drizzle full-strength color from a pipette or flick water from a brush to give further patterning.

Finally, brush a full-strength color along each edge to color under the pegs, moving them slightly if necessary. Allow the silk to dry naturally before unpegging it from the bamboo canes.

9. Pin an area onto the regular frame with silk pins, or stretch an area into an embroidery hoop. Place the pattern motifs under the silk and trace out the patterns in outliner. Once the outliner has dried, paint in the motif using a small brush and full-strength silk paints. Allow this pattern to dry before unpinning and restretching the silk to work another area. Continue until outlined designs have been applied across the whole sarong.

10. Tape the silk onto some plastic sheeting to hold the edge taut. Select a heat-fix outliner (not a clear one as it will wash out) and apply a generous freehand line along the whole edge. While the outliner is still wet, brush out the line to spread the outliner slightly. Don't worry if it looks a little messy at this stage (see the project on page 62).

11. Allow the outliner to dry. Then, using a sharp pair of scissors, trim the edge, cutting through the middle of the spread line to form a neat, no-sew edge. Repeat at the other end. Use an iron to heat-fix the whole sarong or set the work by dry-curing in an oven (see page 15).

Using Clear Resist on Colored Silk

Equipment and Materials

- Pongee or habotai silk scarf
- Frame and silk pins
- Steam-fix colors
- Water pot and mixing palette
- Paintbrushes and sponge brushes
- Clear outliner
- Hairdryer
- Peacock feathers or patterns
- Steam-fixing equipment
- Template (page 105)

Feathers come in all shapes, sizes, and colors, and the peacock feathers in this project have been drawn directly from feathers placed underneath the silk. Use the feather patterns at the back of the book if you do not have any real ones. By initially painting the background in a pale color, and using only clear outliner for the feathers, the resist lines will not show in the completed piece, provided the background is not repainted. Use diluted colors for the background so that the clarity of the colors in the feathers will not be adversely affected.

Pin the silk scarf to the frame with silk pins. Prepare the colors for the background by diluting them with water in a large palette well. Apply the background colors across the whole of the scarf, using a sponge brush. Create a smooth or slightly textured pattern with soft watermarks by adding water or more color while the ground is still wet. Dab all of the outer edges with a piece of kitchen paper to remove any excess paints and to prevent dye from flowing back from the rolled edges. Allow it to dry naturally.

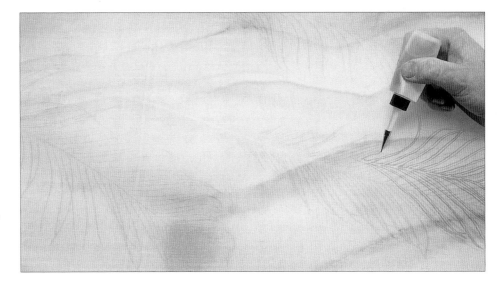

2. Place the peacock feathers or patterns under the painted silk. Look through the silk and trace off the pattern in clear outliner. Remember that the outliner will not show in the completed work, so do not worry about blobs or heavy outlines.

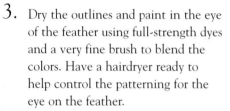

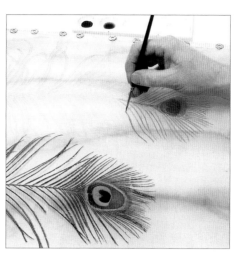

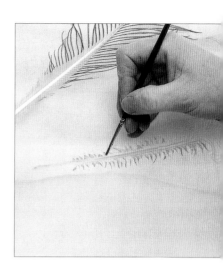

3. Dry the outlines and paint in the eye of the feather using full-strength dyes and a very fine brush to blend the colors. Have a hairdryer ready to help control the patterning for the eye on the feather.

4. Use a fine brush and carefully continue painting in the feather. Use several colors to give shading and depth to the piece.

5. Now paint in and shade the quill of the feather. When all of the feathers are painted, steam-fix the work in the usual way and then wash the silk to remove the outliner. Iron while the silk is still just damp to restore the full sheen and drape of the silk.

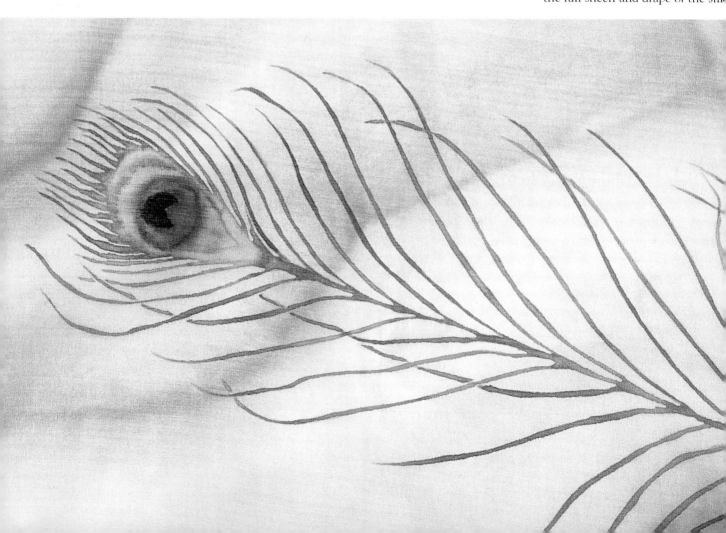

Velvet Evening Bag

Equipment and Materials

A piece of white silk-viscose velvet

A selection of steam-fix dyes

Discharge viscoser, salts, and effect colors

Selection of large paintbrushes or sponge brushes

Mixing palette and water pot

Kitchen roll

Piece of plastic to protect your work surface

Rubber gloves

Masking tape

Permanent pen and bag pattern

Steaming equipment

Hot-stamping blocks and printing blocks

Iron

Spray bottle with water

Plexiglue and granular beads

Decorative liners

Needle, thread, scissors, and other sewing items to make up the finished bag

Template (page 106)

Show off your silk-painting skills by working this attractive evening bag that incorporates dyeing, discharging, and surface-decoration techniques. Use either steam-fix or procion dyes, although steam-fix dyes are probably best because the discharging medium also requires steaming.

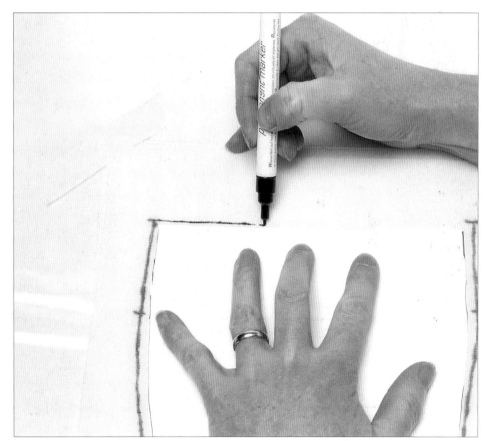

1. Lay the velvet pile side down on the plastic and hold in position with masking tape. Draw around the paper pattern in a permanent-marker pen to allow you to work patterns to fit the shape of the bag, which is made from three pieces.

2. Use large brushes to apply and blend the steam-fix dyes to the back of the velvet. Allow to dry.

3. Pour 1¹/₂ fl oz (30 ml) discharge viscoser into a dish, add ³/₄ teaspoon of magic salts, mix thoroughly, and divide this discharge medium between three dishes.

4. Lift up the uncolored discharge medium from one dish with a pipette, drizzle it onto the pile side the velvet, and dry with a hairdryer

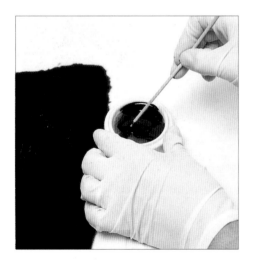

5. Add about ¹/₂ fl oz (10 ml) of effect color to two of the dishes and mix again to make two different-colored discharge pastes.

6. Apply some colored discharge medium to a stamping block.

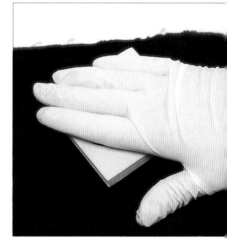

7. Print onto the pile of the velvet inside the pen line. Dry with a hairdryer.

8. Roll up the dry velvet in absorbent paper and steam to set the steam-fix dyes and activate the discharge process. (See page 16 for information on steaming.) Wash the fixed velvet in warm water to remove the spent discharge medium and any excess dyes. Allow to dry a little. Then iron on the reverse, following the lie of the pile.

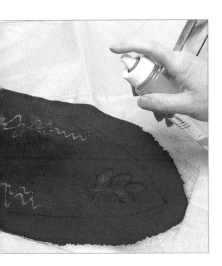

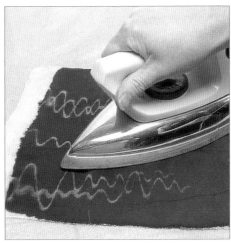

Work some hot blocking or stamping with either hot-potato, rubber stamps, wooden print blocks, or your own lino shapes. Place the block, pattern side up, on the ironing board, then place the velvet pile side down on the block. Spray a little water on the reverse of the velvet.

10. Place a flat iron on the fabric and block and hold it there for 15 to 20 seconds.

11. Carefully peel back the velvet to reveal the pattern imprint. Continue this process across the velvet.

2. Apply a fine line of plexiglue to highlight some areas and sprinkle tiny granular beads across the wet glue lines. Allow the glue to dry completely before removing any loose beads. When dry, add fine glitter lines to accent other areas. Allow all pattern mediums to dry completely before making up the bag. Place the right sides together and sew them up, leaving the top open to turn and add a lining of painted or dyed habotai silk. Finally, add cording or beaded tassels.

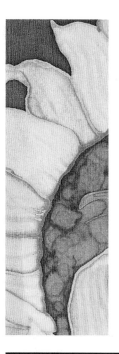

Sunflowers Drawn Using Colored, Water-soluble Outliners

Creating outliners to blend with the coloring of the flowers, or using precolored, water-soluble outliners, gives a design a softer, less stenciled appearance. The completed work is not stiffened, and the movement of the dyes can be controlled as they are painted onto the silk in the normal way.

Equipment and Materials

Ready-edged scarf or piece of silk

Frame and silk pins

Steam-fix dyes

Clear, water-soluble outliner

Precolored, water-soluble outliners

Pipette applicator bottles and nibs

Mixing palette and water pot

Paintbrushes

Pattern

Steam-fixing equipment

Template (page 107)

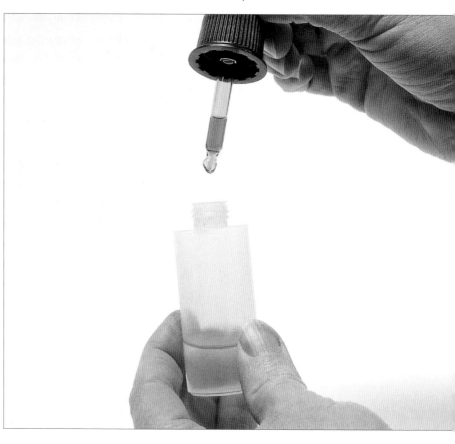

1. Pin the scarf to the frame with silk pins and arrange the patterns under the silk. Pay attention to the shapes and spaces created. To make your own colored outlin[e] pour a little clear outliner into a pipette bottle and add a few drops of dye at a ti[me] until you have an acceptable color and consistency. Too much color will create a[…] runny outliner medium. Try using dye that has become more concentrated after i[t] has dried a little in the palette. Screw a fine nib onto the tip of the applicator bottle. Alternatively, use precolored, water-soluble outliners.

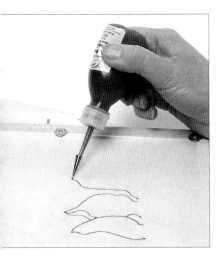

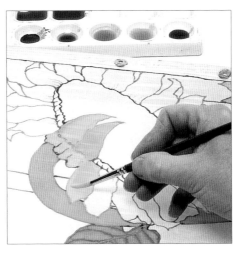

Look through the silk to follow the pattern and draw out the design using the selection of outline colors that you feel appropriate. Allow the outlines to dry, or use a hairdryer, before painting in any of the shapes.

3. Using an appropriately sized brush, carefully paint in the flowers, stems, and leaves.

4. Use shading and blending techniques to give depth to the design and make watermarks to create further patterning.

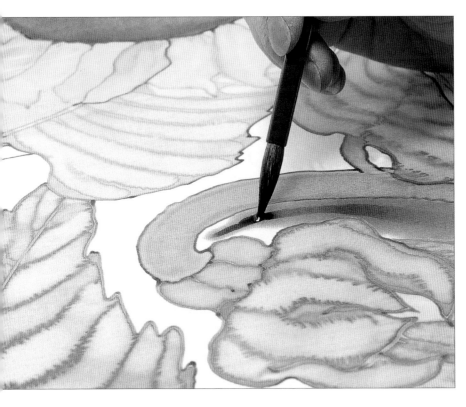

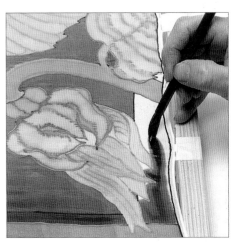

Before painting in the background area or borders, consider a variety of different color options. Then mix up sufficient color to complete each area. Paint in the background and border areas using a combination of large and small brushes to reach all of the nooks and crannies.

6. Remember to work the border alternately, from one side to another, to avoid a join mark.

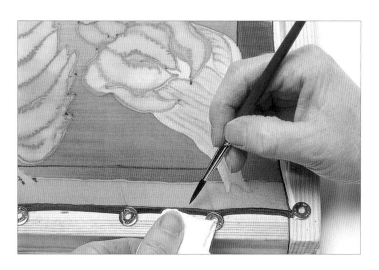

7. Dab the border-rolled edges to prevent flow back. Allow the piece to dry naturally before unpinning and steam-fixing the scarf.

8. Wash the fixed scarf in warm water to remove all traces of outliner. By feeling with your fingers as you wash, you should be able to tell when the glutinous, water-soluble outliner medium has gone. Allow the silk to dry a little before ironing.

Using Silk-paint Thickener to Form a Hand-painted Design

Equipment and Materials

A ready-edged scarf

Frame and silk pins

Steam-fix dyes

Steam-fix silk-paint thickener

Mixing palette and water pot

Paintbrushes

Paper toweling

Hairdryer

Steam-fixing equipment

As you become more proficient with your brush skills, you may like to try working freehand. You don't have to be able to draw pictures to do this, just keep it simple and work an abstract design using straight and curving lines, with dots and dashes formed by the brushstroke. Remember, working with the thickener still provides a good element of control when it comes to the painting. It's fun and gives a real sense of achievement and satisfaction if you are not too confident about working freehand.

1. Attach the silk to the frame using silk pins. Place some silk-paint thickener into the empty palette wells. Add an equal amount of dye to the thickener and thoroughly mix the two together to form a paint medium. Repeat this process for each color to be applied as a thickened medium. Use a firm brush to apply the colors in simple, sweeping shapes across the silk. Allow the shape of the brush to dictate the edge quality of the lines.

2. Allow the thickener pattern lines to dry. Vary the types of brushes used and try working with a double-color-loaded brush for extra variation on the coloring. Leave some areas to paint.

3. Use a paint brush to apply the color a little distance away from the edges of the brushed pattern lines, allowing the dye to flow to these shapes. Work blocks of color, or shadir and patterning, as you wish with the liquid dyes

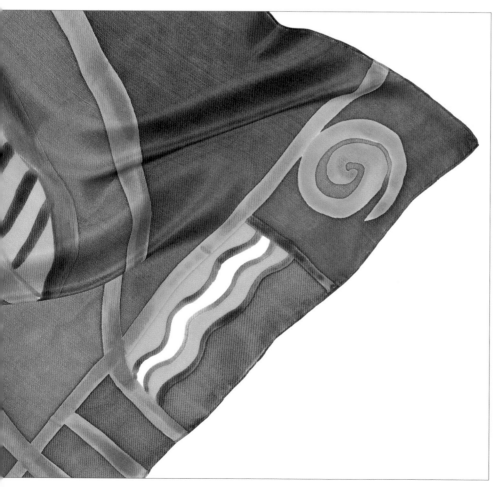

4. When the work is complete, remov it from the frame and steam-fix the dyes. Once the design is fixed, wash the silk in warm water to remove th gelatinous thickener and excess dye As you wash the silk, feel with your fingers to tell when all traces of thickener have been removed. Allo the silk to dry a little before ironing to finish.

Pillow Worked With a Wax Resist

Equipment and Materials

Ready-made, open-sided pillow
frame and silk pins

Wax and wax pot, or double
saucepan and thermometer

Selection of cantings (tjantings)
and brushes

Steam-fix dyes

Brushes for the silk dyes

Mixing palette and water pot

Paper toweling

Patterns

Iron

Newspaper to cover table

Template (page 108)

Working with a wax resist is quite different from working with water-soluble outliners as the wax forms a true resist that permits color washes to be applied over lines and areas already waxed out. Extra care should be taken when working with hot wax, and ideally you should have a thermostatically controlled wax pot or thermometer to check the temperature. Never leave the pot unattended while it is switched on. Please read the safety advice given on page 21 if you have not used wax before.

Tip: if you want to create a crackle effect, brush wax over the whole piece, unpin, and place the waxed silk in a freezer for 10 minutes. This cools the wax and helps to give good crackling. Gently squeeze the silk to form cracks in the wax. Then repin the silk onto the frame and brush a dark color across the whole piece. The dark silk dye will run into the cracks and give a batik appearance to the completed work.

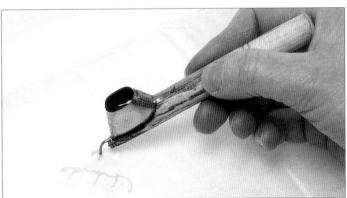

1. Cover the table with newspaper and stretch the silk on the frame using silk pins. Heat the wax to a working temperature of 266°F/130°C. Place the patterns under the silk and allow the cantings to warm through in the wax pot before using them.

2. Using the pattern as a guide, wax in a few details, which will retain the white color of the fabric. Hold a piece of paper toweling against the canting spout to stop the flow of wax and prevent drips as you top up with new hot wax. (See page 21 for tips on applying wax.)

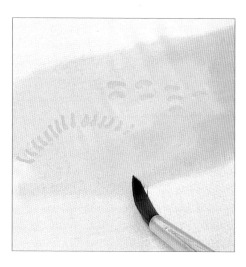

3. Brush the first diluted colors as a pale background wash right over the first layer of dry wax.

4. Use the brush to blend the colors or to add any textural patterning. If you use a hairdryer to dry the colors, make sure that it is not too hot or it will remelt the wax and spoil the design.

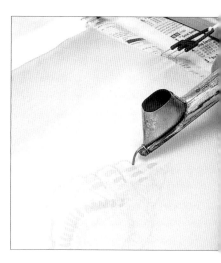

5. Work a second layer of wax, adding more detail to the pattern. This waxing will retain the colors over which it is applied.

6. When the wax is dry, add further color to the shells.

7. Continue waxing in the design and adding color to create a range of patterning and coloring effects.

8. Now draw wavy lines in wax across the whole piece to create a background pattern.

. Paint in all of the stripes to color the background.

Variations: heat-set paints can be used if you prefer, although they will not flow so readily in the subsequent layers, but ironing to remove the wax will also set the paints.

10. Remove the silk from the frame and iron the whole piece between several sheets of absorbent paper or newspaper to remove the wax before steaming the piece in the normal way to set the dyes.

11. Wash the silk in hot, soapy water to remove any final traces of wax and iron once again while just damp to give a good finish. Make up the pillow by sewing along the three open edges, remembering to leave the zip open slightly to allow easy turning through to the right side.

Seascape Picture

Painted silk pictures are an excellent way of displaying the variety of effects that can be achieved with silk paints. The vibrant colors and wonderful patterns just seem to glow on the silk fabric. Seascapes or landscapes are great fun to work, using watermarks to imply features. You don't need a pattern, just allow the work to develop as you work. This project uses antispread to help to control the flow of the dyes without the use of outliner.

Equipment and Materials
Piece of habotai silk
Frame and silk pins
Steam-set silk dyes
Antispread
Paintbrushes
Water pot and mixing palette
Hairdryer

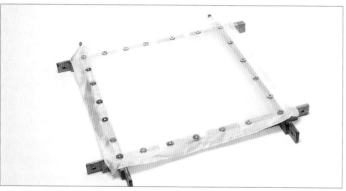

1. Fasten the silk to the frame with silk pins.

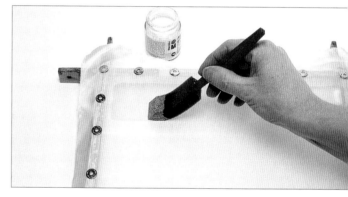

2. Apply a layer of antispread to the silk with a large brush and allow it to dry while you prepare the colors, diluting some with water for paler tints and washes.

3. Draw in the horizon with a rule and a fine brush holding just a little dye. The wet color will not run on the treated silk.

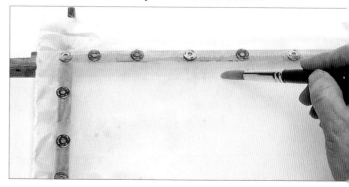

4. Start with the sky, applying a light wash of sky colors over the area. Use water to retain any cloud area as white.

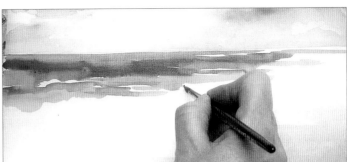

. Allow this to dry, then repeat with slightly darker colors to add depth. Create a layered effect by repainting a few areas, or rewet the whole area to blend in the darker tones. The dyes will not run on dry areas of silk.

6. Repeat this process with the sea, using slightly darker colors, again working in layers, allowing each layer to dry before adding another to create the impression of waves. Any colors applied wet-on-wet will still blend if you want a more shaded effect, or use a hairdryer to dry areas quickly.

. Continue building up the design, working wet-on-wet for blended colors and wet-on-dry to form layers.

7. Use water to dilute the colors and help to blend the beach area with the edge of the waves, working wet-into-wet.

. Working wet-on-dry, add small pebbles and seaweed to the beach and some rays coming down from the sun to create a depth to the picture.

0. When the design is complete, remove the silk from the frame and steam to set the colors. Mount the work in a frame to enhance the completed picture.

Velvet Pillow Using Discharge Paste and Illuminants

This project uses a simple screen-printing technique worked on black velvet, using a discharge paste to bleach out the black. Illuminants provide color to create a beautiful, animal-print effect.

Equipment and Materials

Black silk-viscose velvet

Frame and silk pins

Discharge paste

Illuminant colors

Screen-printing frame stretched

with screen mesh

Squeegee

Masking tape

Plastic sheeting

Plastic gloves

Steaming equipment

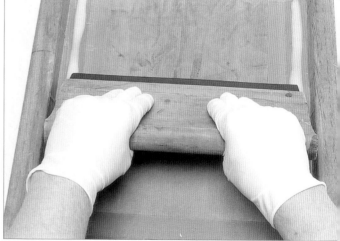

1. Cover the table in plastic and lay the black velvet pile side up on the table. Arrange the velvet into a series of loose folds or pleats. Put on the plastic gloves.

2. Place the screen-printing frame on top of the velvet and pour a good quantity of discharge paste, without any added color, into the top trough edge of the frame. Use a squeegee to pull the discharge paste down and through the screen mesh. It may be easier if someone holds the frame while you do this. Take the squeegee back across the frame several times until all of the discharge paste has been worked through the mesh.

Remove the frame, open up the velvet, and dry with a hairdryer.

Roll up the work and steam (see page 16) to activate the discharge process. Areas to which discharge paste has been applied will turn pale brown, while the areas treated with illuminants will take on new color.

Wash the work in cool water to remove the spent discharge paste and allow to dry a little before ironing on the reverse side of the velvet, following the lie of the pile. Make up into a pillow, adding braiding, tassels, or surface decoration if you wish.

4. Pour a further quantity of discharge paste into a dish, add $\frac{1}{4}$ to $\frac{1}{2}$ teaspoon of yellow illuminant powder, then mix thoroughly.

5. Rearrange the black velvet, pile side up, into a series of new folds, trying to get different areas to work on. Place the screen back on top of the velvet and pour the colored discharge paste into the top trough of the screen. Use a squeegee to pull this across and through the screen mesh. Open up the velvet and dry with a hairdryer.

Devorée Scarf With an Abstract Design and Decorative Foils

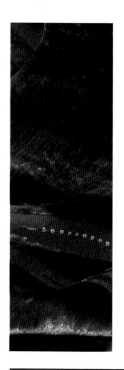

This simple pattern is a good project with which to practice the devorée process and can be worked using steam-fix or procion dyes. The simple lines can be highlighted further with decorative foils. The design is formed from brushstrokes, so a pattern is not required.

Equipment and Materials

A long length of silk-viscose velvet

A selection of either steam-fix dyes or procion dyes and soda ash

Mixing palette and water pot

Large paintbrushes or sponge brushes

Masking tape

Fiber-etch fluid

Paper toweling

Plastic sheeting

Plastic gloves

Hairdryer

Iron

Decorative foils and plexiglue

1. Cover the table with plastic and hold the velvet, pile side down, taut with masking tape. Select a range of colors in your chosen dye and remember to add soda ash to the dye if you are using procion dyes (see page 38). Use large paintbrushes to apply the dyes in broad strokes across the backing of the velvet. Build up the color, blending and overlapping as you go, until the whole length is colored. Do not worry about watermarks showing on the backing because they will not show on the pile side.

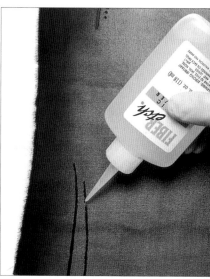

2. Allow the colors to dry, then steam if using steam-fix dyes or allow the work to cure if using procion dyes. Wash and dry the fixed velvet, restretch it, and tape it back into position on the table, pile side down. Apply the fiber-etch solution as evenly as you can, directly from the nozzle on the bottle (see page 39 for information on the devorée process, picking out areas that you wish to highlight with a devorée effect.

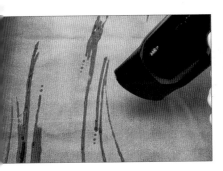

Dry the fiber etch with a hairdryer.

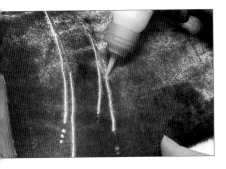

4. Then carefully iron all areas treated with the fiber etch, with the iron set at silk/wool, until the fiber etch has turned pale brown.

5. Check that the pile will release by gently rubbing ironed areas with a finger, then wash the velvet in warm water to release all of the pile and reveal the devorée pattern. Dry the

. Lay the dry velvet out, pile side up, and apply plexiglue to any areas that you wish to highlight with decorative foils. Allow the glue to dry. It will then become transparent.

. Lay a piece of decorative foil, color side up, on the transparent glue line and gently press the foil to transfer the color. Continue until all of the glue lines have been foiled.

. Make up the scarf by placing the right sides together and tacking along the edges before sewing, leaving a small opening to allow for turning through. Close the opening with a few stitches once the scarf has been turned right side out.

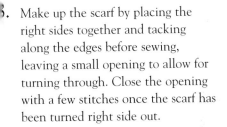

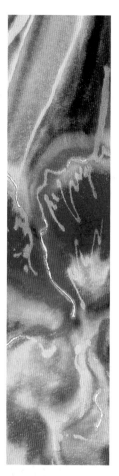

Painted Devorée Velvet Scarf With Foil Highlights

This scarf is worked in a similar way to the previous project, but the floral pattern is painted, working the design freehand or from guidelines drawn in with a vanishing water-soluble pen.

Equipment and Materials

Length of silk-viscose velvet

A selection of either steam-fix dyes or procion dyes and soda ash

Mixing palette and water pot

Large paintbrushes or sponge brushes

Masking tape

Fiber-etch fluid

Kitchen paper

Plastic sheeting

Plastic gloves

Vanishing pen and pattern (optional)

Hairdryer

Iron

Decorative foils and plexiglue

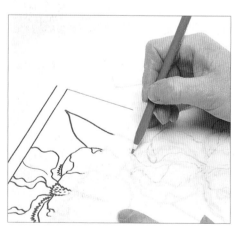

1. Cover the table with plastic and hold the velvet, pile side down, taut with masking tape, with the pattern sheet under the velvet if you want to trace out the lines with a vanishing pen. You can also use the pen to give a few guidelines when working freehand. All pen lines will disappear once the dyes are applied.

2. Use large paintbrushes to apply the dyes (remember to add soda ash if using procion dyes). Use overlapping strokes to mix and blend the colors as you work, and use a hairdryer to help control the flow of the dyes.

3. Use water to keep any areas white pale and start painting in the flowe heads first. Just use the tip of the brush to help achieve fine control the pattern where necessary.

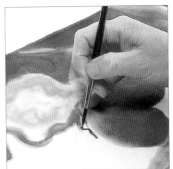

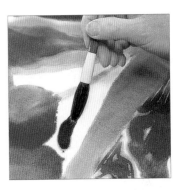

When the flower heads are painted, brush in the leaves and stems. If the flowers are still wet, it will help to prevent the flow of dye into these areas, otherwise control the spread of the dye using a smaller brush and less brush contact with the velvet.

5. Paint in the background. Leave a good spreading distance, otherwise the background color will swamp the pattern.

6. Add a little of the violet and green from the flower colors to give the dark background more depth.

7. Allow the colors to dry, steam if using steam-fix dyes, or allow the work to cure if using procion dyes. Wash and dry the fixed velvet, then restretch and tape it back into position on the table, pile side down. Apply the fiber-etch solution as before (see page 96), using the devorée process to highlight parts of the flowers and leaves.

8. Add decorative-foil highlights with plexiglue, as described on page 97 (or see page 49).

. Make up the scarf by placing the right sides together and tacking along the edges before sewing, leaving a small opening to allow for turning through. Close the opening with a few stitches once the scarf has been turned right side out.

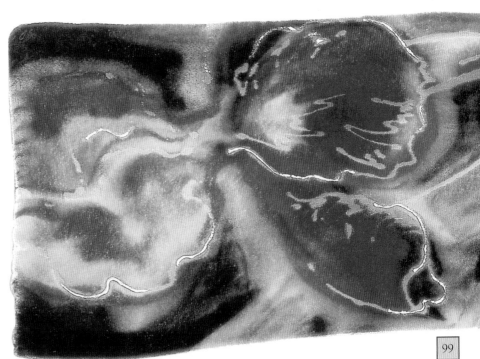

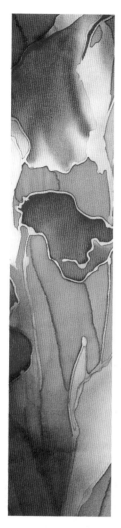

Working With Washes, Watermarks, and Minimal Resist

This project requires much more skill in handling and applying the dyes because the control element comes from the way the colors are allowed to spread, rather than controlling the spread of the dye with resist mediums. The pattern is built up in a series of layers. Because minimal resist is used, the pattern continually develops and watermarks form as further color is applied to already painted areas. The finished result is worth the effort as it gives a beautiful, watercolor appearance to the work.

Equipment and Materials

Ready-edged silk scarf

Silk-painting frame and pins

Steam-fix dyes

Clear, water-soluble outliner

Mixing palette and water pot

Paintbrushes

Paper toweling

Hairdryer

Steam-fixing equipment

Template (page 109)

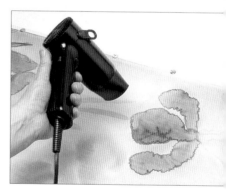

1. Pin out the silk using silk pins and place the selected colors into the mixing palette, diluting them with some water. If you feel unsure about working freehand, place a paper pattern of a flower head under the silk as a guide, rather than a pattern to be rigidly followed. This will allow the design to evolve as you work.

2. Using the diluted colors, roughly paint in the flower heads, positioning them at varying heights and spacing them so that they are at the top, bottom, and edges of the scarf. Now add soft background colors across the whole piece, letting them blend wet-into-wet.

3. Allow the work to dry, then start adding more detail to it, repainting the flowers with deeper colors and adding some leaves and stems, using careful brushwork and a hairdryer to help control the spread of the dyes. Continue layering up the design, reworking areas and creating watermarks as the new layers displace earlier, dry layers of dye.

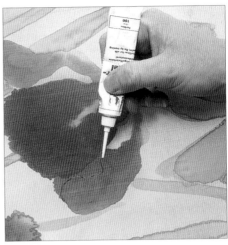

To work more detail into the design, create deliberate watermarks to form leaves and stems, but remember that the leaves first painted in will be in the background and, once dry, further leaves painted on top of those already painted will appear to be in the foreground. Before reworking areas, check what impact they will have on the whole piece as you may form watermarks in the wrong places.

5. Use a little clear outliner to add sharper definition or to give tighter control over the movement of the dyes in areas that you do not want to disturb.

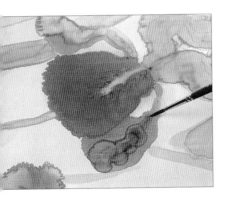

. Continue building up the design until you are happy with the result.

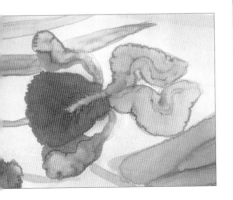

. Dry, then steam, the completed piece, and wash and iron in the usual way to finish.

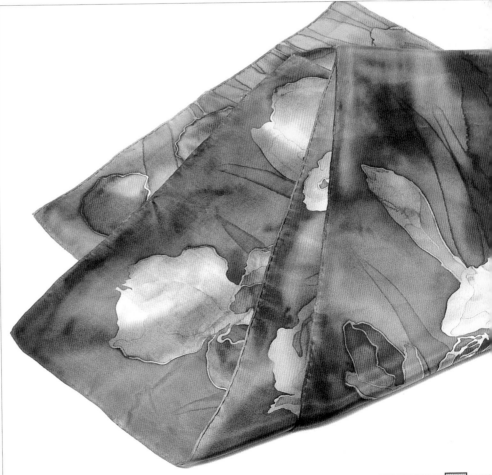

Templates

Freesia Scarf
Increase by 200%

lk-painted Cards
crease by 200%

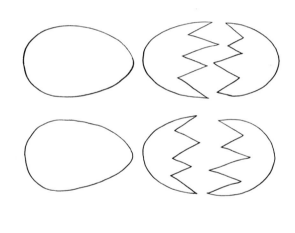

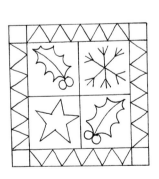

Silk Sarong
Use at this size

sing Clear Resist on
olored Silk

crease by 200%

Velvet Evening Bag
Increase by 133%

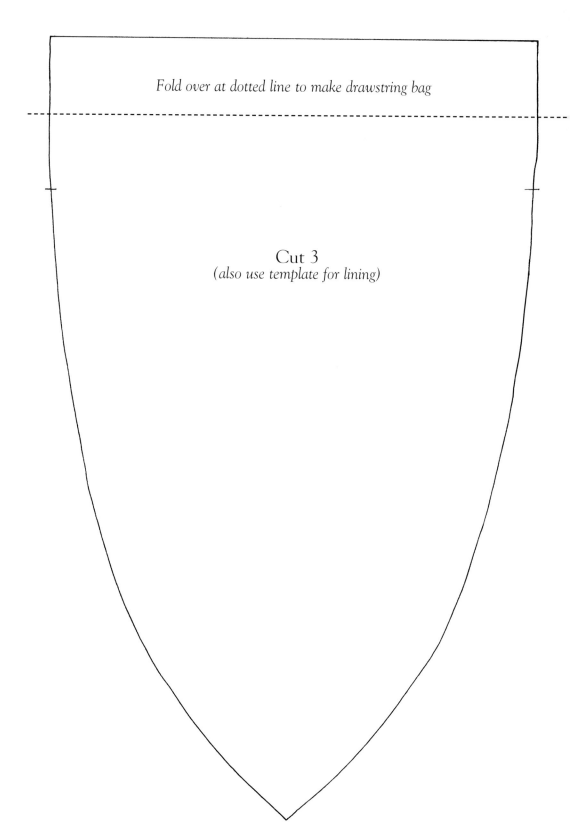

Fold over at dotted line to make drawstring bag

Cut 3
(also use template for lining)

unflowers Drawn Using Colored, Water-soluble Outliners

crease by 300%

Pillow Worked With a Wax Resist
Increase by 133%

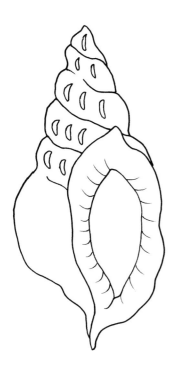

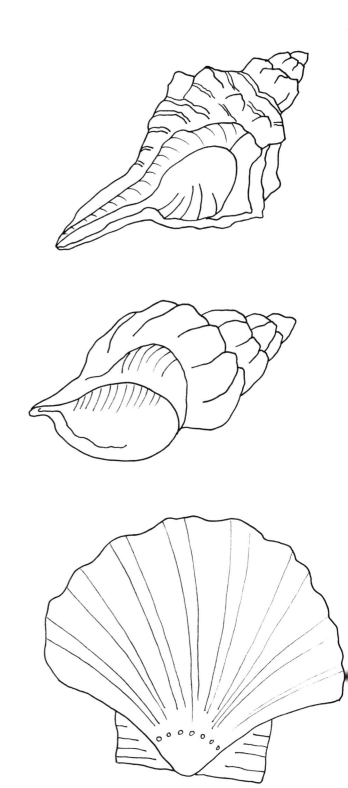

inted Devorée Scarf
orking With Washes, Watermarks, and Minimal Resist
rease by 300%

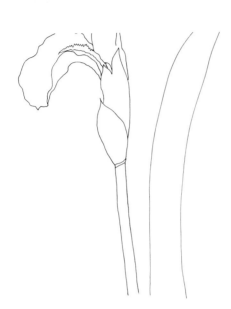

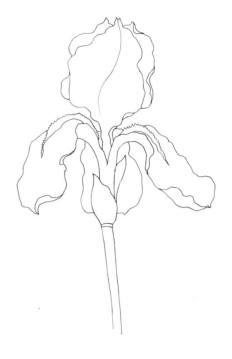

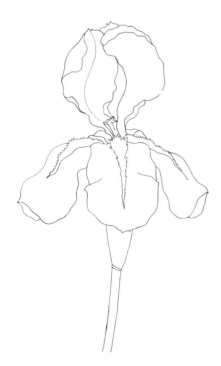

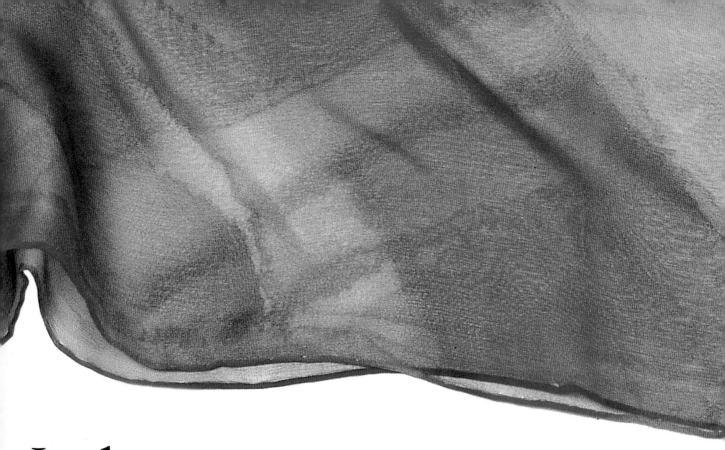

Index

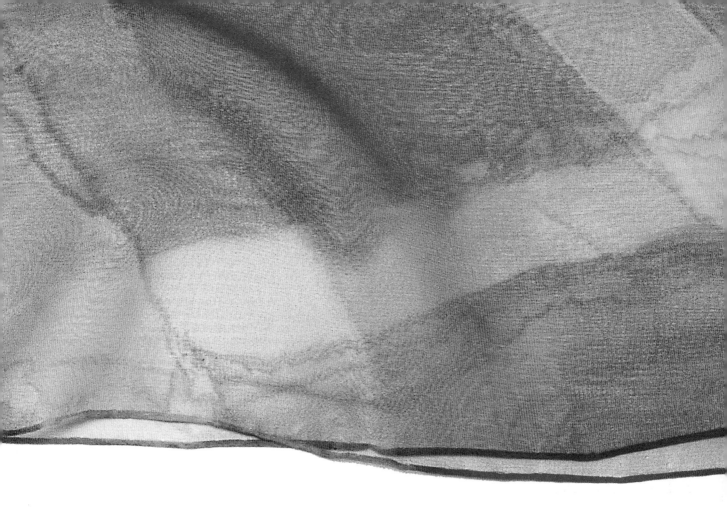

Credits and Acknowledgements

I would like to thank my family for being so supportive to me whilst I was writing this book, and the following suppliers who generously gave materials and equipment for use and illustration in the production of this book.

Edding (U.K.) Ltd., Merlin Centre, Acrewood Way, St. Albans, Herts, AL4 0JY., U.K.
Rainbow Silks, 7 Wheelers Yard, High Street, Great Missenden, Bucks, HP16 0AL, U.K.
Specialist Crafts Ltd., P.O. Box 247, Leicester, LE1 9QS, U.K.